MW00719394

Jewelry & Gems
for Self-Discovery

About the Author

Shakti Carola Navran is from Cologne, Germany, where she attended art school and was also trained in the traditional European apprenticeship system by master jewelers, attaining the rank of journeywoman. She owned an art gallery in Cologne for seven years and began her independent practice as a jeweler in her gallery.

In Germany she also began her lifelong study and practice of astrology and many other spiritual traditions and practices. She has been an astrologer for thirty years and has given readings all over Germany. She continues to explore new spiritual practices today. She now makes jewelry at her studio in Maui, Hawaii.

Shakti's beautiful jewelry may be viewed at her website, www.shakti jewelry.com

To Write to the Author

If you wish to contact the author or would like more information about this book, please write to the author in care of Llewellyn Worldwide and we will forward your request. Both the author and publisher appreciate hearing from you and learning of your enjoyment of this book and how it has helped you. Llewellyn Worldwide cannot guarantee that every letter written to the author can be answered, but all will be forwarded. Please write to:

Shakti Carola Navran
c/o Llewellyn Worldwide
2143 Wooddale Drive, Dept. 978-0-7387-1443-1
Woodbury, MN 55125-2989, U.S.A.

Please enclose a self-addressed stamped envelope for reply,
or $1.00 to cover costs. If outside U.S.A., enclose
international postal reply coupon.

Many of Llewellyn's authors have websites with additional information and resources. For more information, please visit our website at:
www.llewellyn.com

Jewelry & Gems
for Self-Discovery

choosing gemstones that delight the eye & strengthen the soul

shakti carola navran

Llewellyn Publications
Woodbury, Minnesota

Jewelry & Gems for Self-Discovery: Choosing Gemstones That Delight the Eye & Strengthen the Soul © 2008 by Shakti Carola Navran. All rights reserved. No part of this book may be used or reproduced in any manner whatsoever, including Internet usage, without written permission from Llewellyn Publications except in the case of brief quotations embodied in critical articles and reviews.

First Edition
First Printing, 2008

Chart wheels on pages 31, 49, and 75 were produced by the Kepler program by
    permission of Cosmic Patterns Software, Inc. (www.AstroSoftware.com)
Cover design by Gavin Dayton Duffy
Cover image © Jeffrey Hamilton/Digital Vision/Punchstock
Editing by Nicole Edman
Illustration on page 11 by Llewellyn art department
Insert design by Jeanette Jones
Insert photography on pages A1–A6 by Henry Mason and Robert Dube,
    except Azurite (A1); Beryl, Heliodor (A2); Bloodstone (A2); Chrysocolla (A2);
    Chrysoprase (A2); Opal (A4); Quartz (A4); and Zircon (A6) by Llewellyn
    Worldwide
Insert photography on pages A7–A12 by Azad Photographer of Art
    (http://www.azadphoto.com)
Interior book design by Joanna Willis

Llewellyn is a registered trademark of Llewellyn Worldwide, Ltd.

Gemstones and crystals are tools to balance your energy and underlying patterns, not to treat medical conditions. If you have a medical problem, please see a doctor. We assume no liability for any use or misuse of the information given here.

Library of Congress Cataloging-in-Publication Data
Navran, Shakti Carola, 1957–
Jewelry & gems for self-discovery : choosing gemstones that delight the eye & strengthen the soul / Shakti Carola Navran. — 1st ed.
    p. cm.
ISBN 978-0-7387-1443-1
1. Precious stones--Psychic aspects. 2. Gems--Psychic aspects. 3. Crystals--Psychic aspects. I. Title. II. Title: Jewelry and gems for self-discovery.
BF1442.P74 N
133'.25538--dc22
            2008020196
s

Llewellyn Worldwide does not participate in, endorse, or have any authority or responsibility concerning private business transactions between our authors and the public.

All mail addressed to the author is forwarded but the publisher cannot, unless specifically instructed by the author, give out an address or phone number.

Any Internet references contained in this work are current at publication time, but the publisher cannot guarantee that a specific location will continue to be maintained. Please refer to the publisher's website for links to authors' websites and other sources.

Llewellyn Publications
A Division of Llewellyn Worldwide, Ltd.
2143 Wooddale Drive, Dept. 978-0-7387-1443-1
Woodbury, MN 55125-2989, U.S.A.
www.llewellyn.com

 Printed in the United States of America on recycled paper comprised of 15 percent post-consumer waste

For my husband Will,
whose presence is my delight.

Contents

List of Tables and Charts   *xi*
Preface   *xiii*
Acknowledgments   *xvii*

1   From the Rhineland to the Island of Aloha:
    My Personal Journey. 1

2   Astrology:
    The Language of the Soul 9

3   The Birth Chart:
    Your Personal Map of the Heavens. 29

4   How to Read a Birth Chart:
    A Basic Interpretation of Melanie's Birth Chart . . .47

5   Astrology and Gemstones:
    Using the Gifts of Mother Earth
    for Personal Growth and Healing. 57

6   Discovering Your Twelve Stepping Stones
    for Transformation 73

7   Guide to Gemstones and Crystals:
    Physical and Metaphysical Properties 93

8   Chakras and Healing Through
    the Rainbow of Colors .145

9   The Metaphysical Aspects of Metals:
    Are You a Gold or a Silver Person? 153

10 Designing the Perfect Piece of Jewelry 167

11 Finding and Empowering the Perfect Piece of
    Jewelry for Your Heart and Soul 175

    A Farewell As You Set Off   185

Tables and Charts

Chapter 3

Melanie's chart ... 31
The 12 Houses & Their Corresponding Life Areas ... 32
The 12 Zodiac Signs and Their Symbols ... 33
The Heavenly Bodies & Their Symbols ... 34
Table of Astrological Signs ... 41

Chapter 4

Melanie's chart ... 49

Chapter 6

Anne's chart ... 75
Signs, Houses, and Ruling Planets ... 76
North Node Gemstones ... 86
Chiron Gemstones ... 88
Gemstones, Star Signs, & Their Planetary Influences ... 89

Chapter 9

Relative Importance of the Planets, Ascendant, & Midheaven ... 162
Distribution of Planets Among the Elements on Anne's Chart ... 163

Preface

Have you ever fallen in love with a crystal, gemstone, or piece of jewelry at first sight? Have you been inexplicably drawn to a work of art or a beautiful object, such as a painting, a sculpture, jewelry, or something in nature? Human art and God's creation both touch our soul in a unique way, to nourish and heal us.

Opening ourselves to the touch of beauty is like receiving a kiss that brings radiance and wonder into our lives. To be sensitive enough to be touched by beauty and love is like drinking a glass of cool, refreshing water, full of clarity and renewed energy.

I notice that when I feel more connected to my true being I am in awe of all the beauty around me. Beauty makes me feel so grateful for my life. Appreciation for beauty helps me to be fully in the present moment; it makes me feel complete and content. Beauty is a precious gift that has the power to transform our lives from a mundane, gray existence into one that is colorful and exultant. I call these gifts from God; others may refer to the divine or the Spirit or use other terms, but the idea of beauty as a sacred gift remains the same.

When I was studying art and jewelry making in Germany twenty-eight years ago, I was unable to connect personally with the art theories that were being taught at that time. My professors talked about art in a way that felt very artificial and abstruse to me. One of them had an operation in which he had a half-inch steel disk inserted into his upper arm. He proudly displayed the x-ray and defined this as a work of art! At that time, I was immersing myself in learning about Egyptian jewelry and couldn't relate at all to this approach to art—devoid of personal and spiritual meaning.

I was left to find my own way in my art studies. The gift in that was that I had to find my own truth about art and beauty and trust my own process of discovery. I received a lot of guidance and support along the way, but it didn't come from the places I'd expected. My journey toward beauty and truth turned out to be a spiritual journey.

In my experience, beauty calls and moves us to the extent that we are willing and able to hear and be with it. My life's work has been to create what I call *Jewelry for the Soul*, or *Soul Jewelry*—objects of beauty and adornment that speak to the unique spiritual qualities and needs of each of my clients. Jewelry for the Soul can be used and appreciated in many ways to enhance your well-being and spiritual growth. This book is meant to give you information about the astrological and healing aspects of crystals and gemstones, so that you will be able to choose a truly magnificent piece of jewelry.

In ancient times, jewelry was always created for the special purpose of empowerment or healing. It was used in religious ceremonies and as an object of power, to channel and enhance specific energies and frequencies. Jewelry stated the power and status of an individual. Through the ages, that might have been a caveman's tiger's claw or a bear's tooth, a medieval king's jeweled crown, or the pope's ceremonial necklaces and rings. In museums we witness the importance of jewelry for native peoples and kings and queens and in the religions of the world. The Catholic Church still uses the power of jewels in its rituals.

Nowadays we seem to have lost those traditions and knowledge in jewelry making. Only a few jewelers still uphold the tradition of using universal wisdom and ancient knowledge of the healing powers of gemstones and crystals to create meaningful jewelry.

I have been a jeweler since 1978 and have engaged in a journey of self-discovery and spirituality from the beginning. My yearning for creating beautiful jewelry with a deep and meaningful personal spiritual connection led me forward on my own path of discovery.

First, I discovered astrology and the potential uses of the universal principles and rules that astrology reveals. Later I encountered different teachers who worked with the healing qualities of gemstones and crystals. Over my years of study and integrating my personal experience with that of my clients and students, I created Jewelry for the Soul. With the help of the individual astrological birth chart, it is possible to find the most healing and consciousness-enhancing gemstones. I find great satisfaction in using these stones to create a custom-made piece of jewelry for my clients, knowing that this unique jewelry touches and enhances the soul on its journey to self-realization.

We feel drawn to the beauty, harmony, and symmetry that nature offers us in the wondrous specimens of the mineral kingdom. Those qualities can be enhanced and utilized by setting gemstones and crystals into beautiful pieces of jewelry according to the principles of universal energy.

I am most grateful for my ability to create beauty that nourishes the soul and enriches life, and I would like to share the beauty and power of the world of gemstones and crystals with you. I hope you will find guidance throughout this book for finding or creating your own piece of Jewelry for the Soul and that you will come to appreciate all that the magnificent realm of gemstones and crystals has to offer for enriching your life.

Acknowledgements

A book is never the doing of one person, nor an isolated life event! A book such as this one comes about through the author's life journey, enriched by the people who impacted that journey and therefore the author's acquired wisdom, so that it might be shared in written form.

And so I would like to express my deep gratitude to all those along my path who in one way or another have brought me closer to the person I was meant to be. Teachers on our life journey come in all shapes and sizes. Very often those who we perceive to be our foes turn out to be very good teachers, and I am grateful to them. Fortunately, I have also had many positive teachers.

I express my thanks to my many students and clients who discovered the beauty of creation together with me. I am especially thankful to my patronesses Sharie Liden, Toby Neal, and Katie Gibson for encouraging and supporting me through their passion for my jewelry.

My special gratitude goes to my friend and editor, Margaret Copeley. Without her magic way with words, her encouragement, and her clarity, this book would not be what it is.

Many thanks to my friend and photographer, Azad, for his great patience in shooting the jewelry photos just as I wanted them.

Thanks to my friend John Elder for his many helpful suggestions.

Finally, I thank my friends in my creative support group, the Frutta Girls, for believing in my vision.

1

❖

From the Rhineland to the Island of Aloha

My Personal Journey

When I begin reading a book I always like to know more about the person who wrote it. I appreciate seeing a picture of the author and reading about the author's life and work. This gives me a sense of who the writer is and gives me a deeper connection with the book.

Creating jewelry from beautiful gemstones is a highly personal spiritual experience for me. In my work I draw deeply on my life experience and what I've learned during my spiritual journey in response to my life challenges. Perhaps reading about how my work grew out of my life course will help you to understand what I strive to achieve in my work, and you will better see how Jewelry for the Soul can help you on your own journey.

My Fascination with Ethnic Jewelry

I spent fourteen years of my early life in Cologne, Germany, the cultural capital of the Rhineland, with its beautiful medieval cathedral, thirty-one museums, and Germany's largest arts fair. When I discovered the museums and all their beautiful collections of jewelry from other

1

times and places on the Earth, I was utterly enchanted and touched by the art from the Egyptians, Etruscan, American Indians, Greeks, Celts, and the Roman Empire. From then on, my own European heritage has greatly influenced my work as a jeweler.

I decided I wanted to pursue a trade that would allow me to be self-employed and express myself creatively. I was drawn to jewelry making for the intimate, personal connection I felt with jewelry: you admire it, enjoy it, and wear it on your body.

Apprenticeship and Studies

In Germany there is a long tradition of apprenticeship in the crafts, reaching back to the Middle Ages. I began my apprenticeship at age twenty-one at a master jeweler's studio in the outskirts of Cologne, working under harsh conditions in a cold cellar. But I was an independent-minded young woman with a vision for my future. After a year and a half, I left my apprenticeship and began studies at Fachhochschule für Kunst und Design in Cologne. I'd miraculously been chosen out of hundreds of applicants for an art and jewelry class of just ten students.

I knew clearly that jewelry making was my passion and my future and I was determined to learn it.

My most important teacher, Mechtild Baumann, was in her forties and an accomplished master jeweler, and I was a young woman of twenty-two in need of a mentor. She befriended me and took me under her wing, and this became a very fruitful relationship. I went to study and work with her at her studio and home in Cologne, and it was Mechtild who taught me true goldsmithing.

Under the medieval guild system, a craftsman became a journeyman upon finishing an apprenticeship. For a period of at least five years, the journeyman would travel from town to town, looking for work with different masters in order to perfect his skills. Only after further training and taking an exam could the journeyman achieve the level of master. In accordance with that long tradition, I signed a new contract with Mechtild, finished out my apprenticeship with her, and successfully passed my final exam to become a journeywoman.

I have precious memories of the time I spent with Mechtild. We were together the entire day, from morning to night. She was my guardian angel and a wonderful teacher. She not only taught me jewelry-making techniques, but opened my eyes and my heart to a deeper level of the craft that had been lacking in my previous training. She had piles of books about ancient cultures and their jewelry making. We would spend the day at the bench with a big pot of tea between us, working, investigating those books, listening to the music of legendary jazz and New Age musician Paul Horn, and discussing the meaning of life.

Finding a Spiritual Path

I was brought up in a religious family—my grandfather was a Protestant minister—and I had a spiritual orientation in life even as a child. I always felt an inner connection to God.

As a Gemini rising, I am compelled to constantly learn about a great many things that awaken my curiosity. That thirst for knowledge took me on a journey that immersed me in spirituality and a quest to understand how I could express my spirituality through my work. Mechtild used to say that her art was her spiritual path. At that time I didn't really grasp what that meant for her, but as I explored my own spirituality through my art, I began to understand. Today I know that sitting at my jeweler's bench with awareness, presence, and openness to my own being is integrating spirituality into my daily life. I feel very connected and joyful in the process of creation. I love feeling connected to something larger than my ego identity.

From my beginning in art school, I had studied symbols and sacred geometry—the spiritual meaning of the patterns found in nature, from the tiniest things to the cosmos—which led me to learn about astrology. Astrology is one of the oldest systems of seeing and interpreting the world through symbols. It is a system of divination, the discovering of hidden knowledge. Astrology opened my eyes to a vast new world.

I also encountered teachers from all over the world who worked with the healing aspects of crystals and gemstones. My first teacher in the area of healing with gemstones was Daya Chocron, who wrote the first book on this topic many years ago. At about that time, I had a very striking experience in a meditation with a Rubellite Tourmaline. I felt an all-encompassing love spreading throughout my body, especially my heart. My being was filled with sweetness and joy. When I later read about the qualities of Rubellite, I was amazed at how accurate my vision had been. This experience opened me up to the metaphysical world of gemstones and my direct experience convinced me of the energy they contained.

Another teacher I was fortunate to meet was scientist Marcel Vogel, an IBM researcher who developed the first liquid crystal displays (LCDs) and went on to investigate the healing properties of crystals and become a well-known healer. He created ways of cutting crystals to enhance their powers for healing purposes. I met him at several seminars and was invited by him to do research at his laboratory in San José, California. This was my first visit to the United States, in the 1990s.

Others I met started out as healers or spiritual teachers and then began to use crystals to enhance transmission of their own healing energy. Some used crystals for meditation or laid them in healing patterns on the body. What I learned from these teachers allowed me to deepen my knowledge of healing and my connection to my own inner being.

Astrology is both a science and an art form. Anyone can learn the science of astrology, but to apply that science to help people understand the forces at work in their lives, it is necessary to develop a degree of psychic skill as well as communication skill to convey those concepts to people who are seeking understanding.

I always knew I could read people very well. I am able to reach down to subtle levels of people, to sense their inner being, who they are. Sometimes I would see images of them in different settings, like past lives. When I give an astrological reading, I tune in through the chart and have a pretty good feel for how it applies to the client. When I began to work with gemstones, I could hold a stone and tune into it and know its qualities and feel them in my body.

During my training as a jeweler I sought to further develop these psychic skills to enhance my art and the lives of my clients. I learned chakra reading (interpreting the energetic imprints in a person's energy field) with psychic healers.

I was passionate about being a jeweler and excited to discover the deeper meanings of jewelry beyond its simple surface beauty. My loose schedule in art school gave me ample time to pursue my own research and my personal spiritual journey.

After five years of study, I passed my final exam and became a certified artist, which enabled me to be self-employed as a jewelry artist in Germany.

Gallery Phoenix

I used to live in an old neighborhood in the center of Cologne. One day on my way home I came across a small shop that seemed to be empty. I thought this might be a wonderful little shop for a jewelry gallery. I christened it "Gallery Phoenix."

The shop took off almost immediately. Six months later I had another jeweler working for me, and then a second one. Two years later I moved next door to a much larger and nicer gallery space and had five employees.

I very much enjoyed both my work and the success of the gallery. What I found most satisfying at my gallery in Cologne was creating jewelry that had deep personal meaning for people. I learned to create Soul Jewelry that connects us to the spirit and deeper level of our soul, where it becomes an expression of who we are as a being. My clients were involved in the process of design and picking out stones for healing, balance, or expansion into higher aspects of themselves. I gave them an astrological reading, showed them their healing stones, and then designed a very personal piece of Soul Jewelry for them.

In the seven years that I owned my gallery in Cologne, I gave about a thousand astrology readings and many seminars all over Germany about using gemstones and crystals to enhance healing and meditation. This afforded me a great deal of experience and feedback from my clients and others who used gems and crystals in their lives. I heard some amazing stories from them. I had very beautiful and deep connections with people I met through this aspect of my work and found many friends.

In 1994, without a specific plan in mind, knowing only that I needed to take the next step on my journey, I sold the gallery to my partner and moved on into an unknown future. I did some traveling around the world, met more spiritual teachers and healers, and did a lot of soul searching and growing.

My search was to understand how the human mind functions, how to heal trauma, and how to recondition ourselves to live deeper lives. I became very interested in Tibetan Buddhism and saw the Dalai Lama and Tibetan lamas. I did not adopt that path, though, because I sensed that it was very complex and foreign to my Western mind. I did Zen meditation retreats, but found those to be too rigid (and hard on my back!). I learned about Neurolinguistic Programming (NLP) and hypnotherapy from masters such as Tony Robbins and Eli Jaxon-Bear, and I presented introductory seminars in NLP myself. I traveled to India several times, learning from a Siddha yoga master teacher in Kerala, South India, and went to the Oneness University near Chennai.

All of these experiences added to my understanding and deepened my own connection with the divine.

Hawaii, Love, and Soul Jewelry

I had been to Maui in 1991 for a seminar and had fallen in love with the island. I returned here in 1995 initially for a sabbatical and to write. Then I met Will, a jeweler who specialized in creating the most beautiful jewelry with natural crystals. I had done some work with crystals in Germany, but in general it is very unusual for jewelers to work with natural crystals rather than cut stones. Happily, my plan to stay in Hawaii for only one year was foiled by falling in love with Will! Our two souls recognized each other instantly. We embarked on a new life and a new business together here on Maui. And that is how I came to live and work in paradise with my husband.

Will and I have been happily living on Maui for thirteen years now, working in our home studio on the slopes of Haleakala Mountain, an ancient dormant volcano. Maui is a truly magical place. Astrologically it is a place of Pluto (transformation) and Venus (love and art). Maui is home to a great variety of artists: our many writers, painters, jewelers, sculptors, and woodworkers find that the island is a conductor that frees creative energies and helps them to manifest their visions.

When I first came here, I was very deeply touched by the spirit and beauty of the island. I am awed by the beauty of nature in all its different forms. From our house we have a view over the West Maui Mountains, surrounded by the ocean, and we watch the most breathtaking sunsets here almost every evening. The colors here are very intense: the blue of the sky and the ocean, the greens of the tropical plants, the bright colors of the flowers. I started painting here with oils and a pallet knife, trying to catch the beauty around me.

Maui is called the island of *aloha*, a Hawaiian word that means "sharing the breath of life." It is a greeting of unconditional love, which I find expressed in the friendliness and close relationships of the people here.

Apprentices have come from all over the world to learn jewelry making with me. It feels good to pass on some of what I have learned and received over the years. Happily, I am back at the bench myself, creating jewelry with my own hands. I have come full circle with the teachings of my most cherished mentor, Mechtild, to find that jewelry making is a spiritual journey and a sacred act.

I create my own jewelry with attention to harmony of form, conscious use of metals, and, of course, colorful combinations of gemstones. I also do personal counseling and Gemstone Profiles for people who are interested in discovering the gemstones that heal, nurture, and support them. Occasionally I lead weekend seminars on Meditation and Healing with Gemstones and Crystals and hold Oneness Deeksha events. You can find all kinds of creations from my heart to yours at my website, www.shaktijewelry.com.

I lead a quiet life where there is time to meditate, sit with my cat, work in the garden, and continue my inner spiritual work, which is most important for me. I feel nourished by the beauty all around me and feel very grateful for where my life's journey has brought me.

In this book, I share with you the spiritual principles and information about gemstones and crystals that have brought beauty, insight, and energy into my own life for over thirty years so that you may engage more deeply and with greater joy in your own life journey.

2

❧

Astrology

The Language of the Soul

Astrology offers tremendous healing potential through deep insights and self-understanding. In this chapter, I will introduce you to the fundamentals of astrology in order to deepen your understanding of why and how astrology can work for you. We will also explore the concepts of enlightenment and higher consciousness and how they can guide us on our spiritual journey.

When you have grasped the basics of astrology, you will understand how the startling beauty and radiance of gemstones can have such a powerful impact on the human mind, body, and spirit as they support us in our pursuit of wellness and growth.

Astrology means "the study of the stars." It is an ancient science that elucidates the laws by which the universe is governed and teaches us how to apply those laws to our lives. Astrology originated with the Egyptians and was greatly refined by the Greeks, who added to it their learning in astronomy and mathematics.

The stars and planets move in cyclical patterns, and human life on the Earth is interconnected with those movements. Astrologers observe the position of the heavenly bodies at the moment of our birth and study the qualities of those bodies and their interrelationship to explain how they influence human affairs and terrestrial events.

I have studied astrology for thirty years and have helped many people understand their lives through its principles. I have come to deeply appreciate the elegance and simplicity with which astrology can reveal to us the deeper mechanics at work within ourselves and in our lives. Astrology gives us a new way of seeing and understanding ourselves and our lives. It teaches us to examine ourselves from a more holistic point of view.

In this book you will learn how the principles of astrology find their expression in the healing and balancing powers of gemstones and crystals. In this chapter we will investigate some basic spiritual ideas and link them to the principles of astrology.

The Language of the Soul: Enlightenment, Love, and Beauty

In the Eastern and Western spiritual traditions, we are considered to be engaged in a journey of evolution that will lead us to a state of enlightenment. In that state, we will no longer identify with our individual personality but will be in an expanded state of consciousness in which we feel we are one with everything in the universe, from a blade of grass to every person on the planet. We will feel an ecstatic connection with the divine.

The Chakra System

The easiest way to understand the potential qualities of different colored gemstones is to know how they tap into our energy field through the chakras. Many people have encountered the term *chakra* through their practice of yoga to exercise and balance the body. But what does it really mean?

In the East Indian Yogic tradition, the chakra system, consisting of sites of energy aligned along the midline of the body from the base of the spine to the head, is important to our progress toward enlightenment. The Sanskrit word *chakra* means "wheel" or "circle." Some psychics who are able to see this subtle level of energy describe the chakras

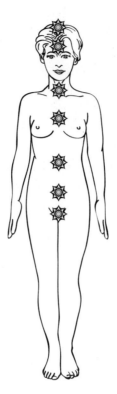

The Chakra System

as turning wheels of colored light. These wheels are like energy transmitter stations, where energy is transferred from a more subtle spiritual level to the physical realm. The chakras act as conductors and connect us to the universal energy that surrounds us.

If the chakra system were completely open and working optimally, we would be fully realized and connected with our divine source. If a chakra is blocked or not fully developed, it creates specific emotional and physical problems. In our evolutionary process of awakening into our full human consciousness, we must work through all the issues connected to each chakra in order to open it up so that it might becomes a perfect transmitter of universal energy for us.

The first chakra is at the end of the spine and is the site of the Kundalini energy, which is described as being curled up like a snake. When the

Kundalini awakens and rises, it makes its way upward, flushing out one chakra after another until it reaches the seventh chakra, where it leads to full enlightenment.

We can look at our development as humans as an evolutionary journey through our chakras. (I will talk more in detail about chakras and their color associations in Chapter 8.) Each chakra stands for a different step in our journey into fully evolved and integrated beings.

The *first* or *root chakra* stands for our identity as a being with a physical body that needs to survive. This is a very instinctual level of being.

The *second* or *sacral chakra* enfolds primary emotions, including our sexual drive.

The *third* or *solar plexus chakra* is where we enter social life, trying to find our place in society, expanding our personal power, and expressing our own creativity and individuality.

The first three chakras represent our animal drives and instincts. This first tier of our development is quite self-centered, being concerned with ourselves, our survival, and our comfort. This is the role of the first three chakras, and these are necessary steps in our evolution. It becomes problematical if we get stuck at this level and our identity does not move beyond this narcissistic stage.

The *fourth chakra* is the *heart chakra*. The first level of the heart opens up when we evolve into higher feelings of love, self-love, and compassion: when we are able to love unconditionally, when we see ourselves in others and feel the oneness in our mutual humanness. The other level of the heart is when we awaken into our true nature—our oneness with the divine—and find our true self.

The *fifth* or *throat chakra* is located in the middle of the throat. Here we learn to interact with the people in the world around us through refining our ability to communicate and to express our personal truth without fear.

The *sixth* or *third eye chakra* is centered in the forehead. When we enter into this level of consciousness, we move beyond the limited individual perspective of the dual world. We feel we belong to a larger consciousness or presence and experience direct knowing and wisdom.

The *seventh chakra* is the *crown chakra* and can be experienced as a golden lotus flower with a thousand petals on the top of the head. This is considered to be the ultimate self-realization of a human being on the journey toward ever higher states of consciousness.

Awakening to Beauty and Art in the Fourth Chakra

When we are dealing with the first three chakras, we don't have much appreciation for true beauty around us because we are so busy with acting from our ego structure, attending to all of our needs and wants. When we come into our heart, these needs have been taken care of. We feel safe and relatively balanced in our ego structure. At that point we can afford to look outside ourselves, to the beauty of the world, in a new and different way. Then we are able to appreciate art, literature, and jewelry. We are open to using our financial resources for things that are beyond immediate survival and ego gratification—things that nourish our soul rather than just our body or personality.

Art has always been for the privileged to some extent. We have to attain some level of abundance before we are ready to appreciate and understand the luxury of art. There has to be a sensitivity of the soul and a longing to be touched and uplifted.

During my five years of art studies, I was confronted with a lot of theory about what art is. All of this talking about art and intellectual theorizing about it felt strange and unnatural to me. Over the years it has become obvious to me that great art needs to touch the heart and our feelings to really impact the soul. For me, art must be able to touch me deep inside and awaken something in me. It makes me thoughtful, opens my mind, and inspires emotions and insights. It inspires me to strive to expand myself, to become my best possible self.

In a way, true art is always from God. The true artist becomes like a hollow piece of bamboo that divine creativity can flow through. True art for me is a process that I partake in, but I am not really the source of it. So it is truly a blessing to be an artist and to be able to be in that flow of the divine.

The art of jewelry should be a call to your heart, to your sense of beauty and love. The heart wants to overflow and share from its abundance and depth. Giving a piece of jewelry can be a statement of love and commitment in a relationship. An heirloom can be given with the idea of passing on wisdom and generosity. Gifting ourselves with jewelry can be an expression of self-love and self-worth. Giving jewelry is always a gesture of abundance and a celebration of love and life.

As the thirteenth-century Persian poet and mystic Mevlana Rumi stated, "Let the beauty we love be what we do. There are hundreds of ways to kneel and kiss the ground." I always feel inspired when I read this and want to find more and more ways in my life to express that love in the beauty I create around me in my life.

I also love this quote from the Indian mystic Osho: "Life is not a problem to be solved, but a mystery to be lived." A beautiful piece of jewelry that touches my soul touches that mystery and celebrates my own individuality, beauty, and expansion of the heart. The gift of magnificent gemstones and crystals is the result of the alchemical forging of Mother Earth, the materialization of colorful light into the physical realm.

The language of the soul is love and the celebration and recognition of beauty in all its expressions.

As Above So Below: The Birth of Alchemy

Alchemy was an ancient science that sought to transmute lead into gold. But that was only the outer layer of the work of an alchemist. His true mission was to transform and transcend the ego in order to attain the highest level of fruition as a true human being.

Alchemy and magic were said to have been founded by the mythical sage or god Hermes Trismegistus, whose divine origins were both Egyptian and Greek. He was believed to have written thousands of texts that were read by the later alchemists. His *Emerald Tablet* was held to contain the secret of the primordial substance of the universe and it later became the foundation of alchemy in the Middle Ages and the

Renaissance. This short text explains the workings of the universe. It is the first paragraph that is of most interest to us:

> This is the truth, the whole truth, and nothing but the truth: As below, so above; and as above, so below. With this knowledge alone you may work miracles. And since all things exist in and emanate from the ONE Who is the ultimate Cause, so all things are born after their kind from this ONE.
>
> The Sun is the father, the Moon the mother; the wind carried it in his belly. Earth is its nurse and its guardian. It is the Father of all things, eternal Will is contained in it. Here, on earth, its strength, its power, remain one and undivided. Earth must be separated from fire, the subtle from the dense, gently, with unremitting care. It arises from the earth and descends from heaven; it gathers to itself the strength of things above and things below. By means of this one thing all the glory of the world shall be yours, and all obscurity flee from you.
>
> It is power, strong with the strength of all power, for it will penetrate all mysteries and dispel all ignorance. By it the world was created. From it are born manifold wonders, the means to achieving which are here given.
>
> It is for this reason that I am called Hermes Trismegistus; for I possess the three essentials of the philosophy of the universe.
>
> This is the sum total of the work of the Sun.[1]

These words are part of what is called the Hermetic Principles and refer to the fact that all universal principles are in operation on all levels of creation. The Hermeticists view the world through analogies—"As above, so below"—rather than through simple events of cause and effect. *The science of astrology is based on this principle*: if I can read and understand the relation of different universal principles on one level of creation, I can apply those principles to all other levels.

....

1 Sadoul, Jacques. *Alchemists and Gold: The Story of Alchemy Through the Ages*. New York: Putnam, 1972.

Using Astrology to Grow into Our Highest Potential

This is exactly what we do with the help of astrology: we observe universal laws and principles in the macrocosm of the planets, and transfer our observations to people, events, or gemstones. By reading the position of the planets and interpreting these universal principles on that level, we can understand other larger or smaller aspects of the universe. For example, we can look at the chart of a newborn baby and discover what this person's potential and life challenges will be. By looking into the planetary forces in effect at this moment of birth, we know what this seed—the beginning of the baby's life—will become.

For example, you can readily observe that a tulip bulb looks very different from the huge seed of an avocado tree. Both contain all the information and material needed for the plants that will grow from them. A tulip bulb will never become an avocado tree. But if you are a good gardener you know what each seed and bulb in your garden will grow into. The good gardener will also know what kind of support, nourishment, water, and sunlight each seed needs to grow into its fullest self.

The same is true for our baby: the baby will only grow into his or her fullest potential if we provide the best possible care. We can't predict the exact events that will happen in this baby's life, but from reading the baby's chart we do know a lot about what kinds of situations will come into the child's life. In the birth chart, we can read very detailed information about what this soul needs in order to grow into its fullest expression and what the soul's challenges and potentials are.

Most of us don't get the optimum nourishment and support we would have liked in our childhood. But at some point in our life we can become our own gardener, responsible for our own growth through the choices we make. The key ingredient here is our level of consciousness.

For me, astrology has proven to be a very elegant and rapid way to obtain an overview of and higher perspective on our personality and our inner design. The astrological chart helps us to step back and look at ourselves and our lives in all their expressions and forms. It can make us more self-aware and give us the power to make important choices about our life path from a higher perspective. Through understanding universal principles and how these are expressed on different levels, a greater range of choices is opened up to us.

The Universal Principles of the Planets and Their Colors

Below are the planets and a brief description of the universal principles represented by each. We will deepen our understanding of their qualities in the next chapter, where we examine the specific concepts and tools of astrology.

Notice here that each heavenly body is represented in the gemstones by a specific color. The color associated with a planet applies to both gemstones and any other use of color in your life.

The Sun represents our self-awareness, our self-identification, our life-force energy, and our vitality. The colors of the Sun in gemstones are yellow, orange, and gold. The heart as our center and the circulatory system are ruled by the Sun on the physical level.

The Moon enfolds the feminine principles of receptivity, nourishment, mother, giving life, receiving and giving, our unconscious mind, fantasy, creativity, safety, and feelings. The gemstone colors of the Moon are white, light bluish, pearly, iridescent, and the silvery hues. In the body, the Moon is connected to the digestive system, bladder, uterus, breasts, and liquids.

Mercury is our intellect, mind, thoughts, flexibility, communication, writing and talking, a mediator between two levels (connecting different things, worlds, and people), teacher, and traveler. The gemstone colors of Mercury are multicolor (many colors occurring together, as in the Opals) and brown. On the physical level, he influences the brain and the nervous system.

Venus, the goddess of love and beauty, represents aesthetics, harmony, Eros, and the beloved. The colors of Venus are pink, yellow, and green. The physical equivalents of Venus are the kidneys, glands, and veins.

Mars, the red planet, is the warrior and conqueror. Mars represents our male physical and sexual energy, our life force, aggression, impulses, will, discernment, and courage. Red reflects the Martian presence in gemstones. In the physical body, Mars is connected with the male genitals, muscle strength, warmth, and the gallbladder.

Jupiter represents our ethical sense, our beliefs and values, our search for reconnection with God, and the principle of expansion. Jupiter, which travels far from the Earth in the outer solar system, is always expanding beyond obstacles such as limiting beliefs and boundaries of countries, opening the mind to deeper meaning. "Expansion" also means wanting to achieve a sense of fullness, which can be expressed in a tendency to overeat! Jupiter's gemstone colors are green, blue, and blue-purple. In the physical body, Jupiter rules the liver and is expressed as excesses, such as obesity and malignant cell reproduction.

Saturn represents the principles of limitation, structure, density, contraction and fear, concentration and crystallization, time and old age. The gemstone colors of Saturn are gray and black. In the body he rules the skeleton, the formation of bones, the skin, and the spleen.

Uranus is the rebel, representing intuition, creative intelligence, an innovative spirit, sudden interruption of continuity, revolution, and change. The colors of Uranus are sky blue and turquoise. In the body, Uranus rules the pituitary gland and nervous system.

Neptune represents unconditional, all-encompassing love, inspiration, the ability to merge (with the divine, others, or anything in the world as an expression of the divine), mysticism, and longing for God—but also illusion, fog, poison, addictions, and weakness. The gemstone colors of Neptune are mauve and purple. On the physical level, the pineal glands and feet are attributed to Neptune.

Pluto represents the principles of transformation, death and rebirth, the phoenix arising from the ashes, regeneration, total change, black and white, extremes, surrender to a higher force, and magic. Pluto's gemstone colors are black or multicolor with lots of red. In the body, Pluto stands for the regenerative forces involving cell formation, the reproductive system, and inherited diseases.

Applying the Planetary Principles to Your Life Path

An astrological view of the world will allow you to perceive these universal principles on all levels of existence: *As above so below!*

I will choose two heavenly bodies, the Moon and Saturn, to illustrate how the planetary principles can be used to understand and change our lives.

As we just saw, the Moon represents the principles of nourishment, mother, giving life, receiving and giving, and our unconscious mind. It represents in general how we feel about life and what we need to feel safe. Saturn represents the principles of limitation, structure (for example, the bones of the body represent the Saturn principle), concentration and density, contraction, fear, and crystallization (both in nature and as a process of becoming clearer). Perhaps you can see how the principles of the Moon and Saturn are not easily compatible. If the two share a hard aspect in a birth chart (you will understand what this means in the next chapter), this will be a challenging merger of principles and the individual will need to discover how to accommodate both aspects. For example, a longing to be nurtured will need to be balanced with a tendency to withdraw in fear.

To continue with our Saturn/Moon example, we might start out life with an overbearing and dominating mother who is not able to nourish and love us to the extent we need. She might feel a high degree of fear of life, which she passes on to us. She might be very controlling and contracted in her own structure. As a result, later in life we may not find it easy to open our heart to others and may feel unsafe doing so. Safety will be a recurring issue. With a Saturn/Moon combination we need a reliable partner, someone we can count on, who is committed.

If we fail to attend to our needs, we may go through life feeling very insecure, shut down, and out of touch with our intrinsic value. We will feel very disconnected and lonely, won't trust anyone, and will never really open up our heart for fear of being hurt—the prototype of the elderly spinster.

But the scenario could have a different outcome. Perhaps because of the limitations we experienced in our childhood and feel now, we might be stirred to investigate the depths of our emotions, conditionings, and personality structures. Saturn wants us to dive into our unconscious. When we do so, we feel the pain of our past and see the connection to who we are today. Only with this understanding will we have positive choices for expressing and balancing the Saturn and Moon principles in our life. Then we can experience the depth and joy of who we are and what we have to give. We may become very creative and giving (mothering) and find ways to express those important qualities, perhaps as an artist, a teacher working with children, or a nurse giving loving care to patients.

The Spiral of Life

The spiral is an archetypal building block of the universe. It can be observed on all levels of existence, from the Milky Way in the macrocosm to our DNA in the microcosm. There are many spirals in nature: whirlpools, hurricanes, the pattern of our hair growth, and many more.

In my twenties, when I started researching symbols, patterns, and forms used in the art and cultural history of humankind, I was fascinated with the presence of the spiral all over the world, in all cultures of all times: it is found in architecture (think of the Guggenheim Museum), painting (from the time of the earliest cave paintings), sculpture, jewelry, and tattoos, and in religious teachings and esoteric scriptures. Here on Maui we have spirals etched into rock formations along with other petroglyphs.

The spiral is such an archetypal pattern, it is so much a part of our consciousness, that it may be an important key to unlocking secret powers and knowledge from the depths of our unconscious mind. It is first and foremost a symbol of life, growth, and evolution. It is a symbol of the journey of our soul as used in the ancient science of astrology.

The cyclical motion of the twelve signs of the zodiac creates a wheel of life, also manifested in the cycle of the seasons. That wheel leads to the next and then on to the next level of expansion and evolution. The spiral is a symbol of eternal evolution, since by design it goes on forever. It symbolizes the growth of our strength and virtues, transcending our animal nature and entering into the highest expression of divine consciousness on the Earth.

The astrological chart represents one circle or cycle of evolution and growth, corresponding to the different seasons of the year. When one circle closes it moves onto the next level, thus creating a spiral.

When we consult an astrological chart we look at one slice taken out of a spiral that is revolving toward the center, toward the point of oneness and wholeness at the center of the chart.

The concept of reincarnation conveys how the soul moves through different stages over many lifetimes, toward its highest human potential. These lives taken together can also be thought of as constituting a spiral turning upward to its highest point. The life that you are living now, with all its karmic potential and burdens, is but one segment of that spiral.

Impermanence and change are the only constants in life that we can count on, and the spiral illustrates that unending cycle of change.

Spiral designs therefore have naturally become an important element of my jewelry. I love their dynamic force, energy, and beauty.

Understanding the Meaning of Our Lives and Our Destiny

Life doesn't make much sense unless seen in a larger context. We may not come to understand the major events that happen in our lives if we look only at the event itself and the pain it causes. Astrology offers us a way of understanding our karma, trials, and challenges in this lifetime by looking for meaning at a higher level.

Our lives are defined in part by our resources and challenges. Resources are areas in our life where we are at ease, where we feel comfortable, know how to react and do things with competence, apply ourselves to life. Challenges are the areas in which we feel reactive and contracted, resist change, perceive ourselves as victims, or experience any kind of trials or suffering. Challenges indicate areas in which we need to grow and expand out of old behavioral patterns. These challenged areas are usually seen in the astrological chart as hard aspects[2] between the planets or the position of the planet in a non complementary sign.[3] In general one can say that all combinations with Saturn, Uranus, Neptune, and Pluto point to a challenge or problem.

Saturn is the guardian of the unconscious and subconscious mind. On the positive side, this protects us from being overwhelmed by its contents, but on the other hand it can block our creativity and access to helpful knowledge and information that we need for our healing and growth. The three outer planets—Uranus, Neptune, and Pluto—represent an open channel to the individual and collective unconscious mind. With this openness there is an inherent sensitivity and the impact of those realms on a person is usually not easy to integrate. We can sometimes see this sensitivity manifested in the fragility of geniuses.

But as we all have experienced at some point, when we really embrace a problem in our life, stop struggling, and surrender, often something new and wonderful may evolve out of a difficult challenge. In that sense it's possible to say that every problem carries a hidden gift. It usually just takes some time to find it. The hidden gift is our destiny, to be discovered and evolved into.

The Moon Nodes and Their Karmic Pull

The apparent path of the Sun across the sky over one year is called the *ecliptic*. The nodes of the Moon are the north and south points where the Moon's orbit crosses the ecliptic. Their projection onto the zodiac shows two points in two opposite signs.

The *south node* is an indicator of where the soul has been on its evolutionary journey, and therefore also what we need to transcend, to move

....

2 A hard aspect occurs when two planets are square (at a 90-degree angle to each other), in opposition (180 degrees), or in conjunction (0 degrees). These are positions of friction that represent challenges related to the principles of the involved planets.

3 For example, fire and water are not complementary. So if Mars (fire) finds himself in Cancer or Pisces (both water signs), this is a noncomplementary position.

beyond. It shows accumulations of all past unresolved issues and the potentials we have at our disposal.

The *north node*, which indicates where we are going, is the magnetic pull of the future and its untried potential for the soul.

The astrological chart is a system of symbols representing reality on different levels. For me the north Moon node ties all the levels of the chart together. It is the bull's eye, where the arrow is aimed before being set into motion. It is our soul's destiny.

It is where our soul longs to go. *It is where our personality doesn't want to go!*

It is very supportive and affirming to work with a gemstone representing that destiny and use its help to move us forward.

Growing into the Fullest Possible Potential in This Life

What is needed for any kind of problem solving is the willingness to look at what is. The willingness to confront our limitations, deficiencies, and vices is the first step of the healing process. The second step is to admit the feelings that are usually connected with those challenges in our character. As you may know, *what we resist persists!*

The second step is usually very challenging for our personality, which is built around avoiding any overloading and threat of "bad" feelings. In our childhood when our personality was forming, it was often essential for our survival that we shut off those immense feelings of hurt, pain, and neglect. So it has become habitual for us to do that, even if we are better equipped today as grown-ups to deal with those feelings.

Our birth chart shows the configuration of the planets at the exact moment of our birth. Studying the characteristics of those planets and the dynamics at work among them can reveal important information about our character and the principles and challenges that come into play over the course of our lives. A good astrological reading can give us an honest look at what is and where we are in our process of coming to terms with our life and our personality. It allows us to take a step back and be curious about who we are in all aspects of ourselves, as of yet integrated or not.

Resource-Oriented Counseling

You should leave a good astrological reading with a sense of awe and expansion of your consciousness. If you feel limited and boxed in by your reading, the information available from your chart wasn't processed in the most advantageous way.

It takes considerable skill and practice to master any profession. This is especially true of working with people, because we can cause more harm by misdirecting someone. Counseling takes a great deal of sensitivity. It is tempting to want to fix people and give them good advice, but true growth arises out of a long process of integration of experience and reflection.

How easy it is to misuse astrological information to limit people, to tell them that because their Pluto is doing this or that, their life is miserable. It is much more helpful to use astrological information to point to the inherent potential of transcendence and growth in a person's chart. But any astrological counseling can only be as good as the state of mind and consciousness of the counselor. I far prefer resource-oriented counseling that focuses on an individual's potential for transformation and better ways to live problem areas. This approach leaves you with a deeper understanding of your personality structure and therefore offers new life choices.

What I like about astrology is the possibility of having a neutral perspective on our personality structure. The planetary principles can be expressed in a variety of ways. When we discover how we have lived out our design so far and what a more evolved way of being would be like, we experience a sense of both destiny and freedom: we come to understand the components of our destiny, and that information allows us to make free decisions about our future.

The Light on the Horizon

Isn't it strange that we humans seem to learn best through pain and struggle? When you look back on your life, you may see that usually you have come out of a difficult time—the end of a relationship, losing your job, uprooting yourself and starting out in a new place—with a new and expanded sense of who you are.

A great deal of suffering arises when we put on the brakes, cling to the old, and reject changes looming before us. Those tactics of resistance never benefit us, but it is such a habitual pattern of defense that we act from a very limited range of choices.

There is within us a deeply ingrained denial of the impermanence of life. It springs from our instinctual need to feel secure. We don't like change because it threatens our need to control our environment in order to avoid feeling fear and anxiety.

Astrology gives us a tool for achieving a deeper understanding of life's challenges and what might be on the other side of those challenges if we face them with courage. It gives us meaning and direction in dark times of the soul. *It points to the light on the horizon that is already inherent in the seeds of our despair!*

A good astrological reading can lighten our journey by giving us a higher perspective on our trials. Sometimes when I merely name those for a client I see a large feeling of relief and relaxation. Simply acknowledging what already is, is the first step for moving beyond our challenges.

When I give a reading I always point out that the reading is just a mirror for what we are able and willing to see of ourselves. A reading should help you to find your own truth and connect with it on a deeper level. So the real purpose of an astrological reading is for you to discern where your own truth resonates with what is presented. You will simply know on a deep level when truth has been spoken by the astrologer. It is also valuable to be curious about presented material that we feel upset about and to reject it if it feels false. If you have a strong emotional reaction to a particular aspect of the reading, this is an indication of an area that merits further investigation and discovery. It doesn't necessarily mean that it is true as presented, but you might find a new and deeper way of looking at yourself.

Our higher consciousness is the best healer and teacher we have. There are many ways of accessing and expanding our consciousness to a higher plane, bringing a new chance to learn and grow without pain. In NLP, it is said that a problem can never be solved on the level where it exists, that we must step up to a "meta level"—astrology, for example—in order to properly see and resolve problems. Therefore any way we can find to connect with our higher consciousness is of great value.

Projection: The Play of Maya

Maya is a Sanskrit word meaning "illusion" or "dream of life." The East Indian (Hindu or Buddhist) perspective is that all of our experience of life is a projection of the mind and therefore an illusion. With the help of astrology we can see very specifically what we project out onto the world and how we perceive the world through our personal filter.

For example, there are two planets that represent the female principles: the Moon and Venus. In the astrological chart of a woman, the Moon and Venus show how she perceives her mother and other women around her throughout her life. Those two planets also represent her own femininity that she wants to find ways to express increasingly in her life. The Moon and Venus in the chart of a man show what kind of feminine representation he is looking for in his life, what kind of woman he will feel attracted to. A man projects out his own feminine side onto the woman of his choice. Sometimes a man's inner image of the female aspect is too different from the outer manifestation in the woman he has chosen and he continually ends relationships, looking for a closer fit.

The same principle holds true, in reverse, for the male principles of the Sun and Mars. Those planets show what qualities a man wants to find within himself, and for a woman what kind of man she is looking for.

To further illustrate the principles of perception and projection, let's examine a stressful Sun/Pluto connection in the chart. The Sun represents our ego identity, father, and self-expression, while Pluto represents transformation, death, or rebirth. Put those two themes together with any important aspect angle and you have a challenge around authority and how you deal with it. If this is your planetary configuration, you will probably have a hard time playing by someone else's rules. One way or another, you will unconsciously create situations with your spouse, boss, friends, and foes in which you feel your values, strength, and will are challenged. Through confronting these situations you have the opportunity to develop your own value independently of the influence of others. You can grow into a person capable of expressing your own power and individuality, and develop leadership qualities. You will know when you have arrived at that level of maturity, because you will no longer feel challenged in the area of authority.

The above examples show how our "cosmic design" creates a perception filter that impacts our choices and actions.

Now that you have a basic understanding of the planetary principles and how they are manifested as resources and challenges in the design of your life, you are ready to become familiar with the other components of astrological thinking in order to gain insight into the makeup of your personality and the main themes of your life.

3

The Birth Chart

Your Personal Map of the Heavens

It takes no particular spiritual beliefs to observe that the swirling cosmos is infused with energy. You yourself are energy and you belong to the cosmos. In fact, you were born of the cosmos! At the exact moment of your birth, the planets—turning on their axes and hurtling through space at speeds of over 100,000 miles per hour!—occupied specific positions in the heavens and their forces came together in a very particular way to create a unique individual, unlike any other person on our planet. Because the entire universe is constantly in motion, one minute sooner or later, those forces were different and would create a different human being. In this sense, you are born of the energy of the heavenly bodies and you will experience their influence throughout your lifetime. Wouldn't it be a good idea to know what those forces are and learn to work with them to achieve your goals?

Astrologers use a symbolic map of the heavens, called a *horoscope*, to show the position of the celestial bodies at the time of any important event, such as your birth. Your personal horoscope is also called your *birth chart*.

How to Obtain and Understand Your Birth Chart

The easiest way for a beginner to obtain a birth chart is to download it for free at websites such as www.astro.com. You will need to provide the date, exact time, and place of your birth. The site will automatically generate a chart of the heavens, showing the positions of the planets at the moment of your birth.

In order for you to make the best possible use of this book, I would like to encourage you to seek a reading of your birth chart from a professional astrologer. An astrologer will untangle the maze of lines and symbols for you, show you where each planet stands, and explain how the planets interact with each other on your chart and what that all means for your personality and your life. Most people find a reading to be an enriching experience, akin to receiving an in-depth narrative from a psychologist who seems to know them surprisingly well! A reading can give you a detailed understanding of your potential, resources, and the challenges awaiting you. Through a reading you will develop an intuitive feeling for the areas in your life in which you need balance and support.

Some competent astrologers such as Liz Green and Robert Hand provide good written readings. These are mostly taken directly from their books and therefore are limited in their depth. I think you will be more satisfied if you obtain a personalized in-person or telephone reading rather than a written interpretation of your chart. A personal reading with an experienced astrologer will allow you to ask questions to obtain clarification of points that puzzle you or that you want to explore in greater depth. A reading with an astrologer will help you to step back from your personality and look at yourself objectively, by using the astrologer as a mirror to look at yourself from a new angle. I'm certain that you will find a personal reading to be the most satisfying way to go about your process of inquiring into your life and your personality.

If you don't choose to have your birth chart read, you can learn about your resources and challenges with the help of the information in this chapter and the next two.

The Basic Elements of the Birth Chart

Now we come to the most technical part of our exploration of astrology. These principles may seem confusing at first, but if you follow the sample chart provided, they will soon make sense. You will then be well equipped to seek a personal reading with a professional astrologer.

The Earth, the Sun, and the Zodiac

The chart below is for Melanie, who was born at 2:15 a.m. on February 11, 1958, in Newport Beach, California. The place of birth is important because the sky looks different from every point on the Earth at any given time.

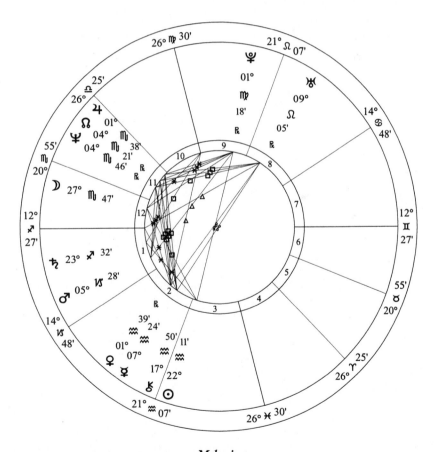

Melanie
February 11, 1958 / 2:15 a.m. / Newport Beach, California

On a horoscope, the Earth appears at the center of the circle, and the heavens are turning around the Earth. The left side of the circle is the eastern horizon, where the Sun rises.

The band of sky surrounding the Earth is called the *zodiac,* a Greek word meaning "circle of animals." The planets move around the sky along this circular path.

The Twelve Houses

The zodiac is divided into twelve *houses,* numbered counterclockwise around the Earth beginning at the point where the Sun rises. The planets are the forces that impact your life. The planets manifest their influence in the houses. The houses represent the important areas of your life as follows:

THE 12 HOUSES & THEIR
CORRESPONDING LIFE AREAS

House	Life Areas
1st	Personality & Self-expression
2nd	Finances & Property
3rd	Communication & Excursions
4th	Home & the Unconscious
5th	Children & Creativity
6th	Work & Health
7th	Partnership & Relating to Others
8th	Death & Regeneration
9th	Higher Mind & the Search for Meaning
10th	Public Image, Career, & Destiny
11th	Friends & Vision
12th	Personal Connection with the Divine & the Invisible Realms

The Twelve Signs

The zodiac is also divided into twelve segments, which are the *signs of the zodiac*. The signs represent energy patterns and modes of expression—how you use the forces of the planets. You can see the signs in the outer ring of the chart.

The signs are named after constellations. Here are the symbols for the twelve signs:

THE 12 ZODIAC SIGNS
AND THEIR SYMBOLS

#	Sign	Symbol
1.	Aries	♈
2.	Taurus	♉
3.	Gemini	♊
4.	Cancer	♋
5.	Leo	♌
6.	Virgo	♍
7.	Libra	♎
8.	Scorpio	♏
9.	Sagittarius	♐
10.	Capricorn	♑
11.	Aquarius	♒
12.	Pisces	♓

You can recognize some of the signs in the symbols, such as the horns of Aries the ram and Taurus the bull.

There is a relationship between the houses and the signs. Each sign appears in a specific house on your chart. For example, on Melanie's chart, Aries is in the Fourth House. The houses don't turn, so they always appear in the same position in the chart. The zodiac does turn, because the heavens appear to be constantly turning about the Earth with each complete day. The signs are always in the same order, but they will be in a different position on the chart according to the time of day. So the signs will be in different houses according to the time of day.

Each house has a corresponding sign that influences it regardless of the time of day. The signs lend their qualities to the houses.

Additionally, each sign is also ruled by a specific planet. For example, Aries is ruled by Mars. The characteristics of that planet (areas of strength and challenge) are therefore associated with the sign as well, so that Aries takes on the qualities of Mars. See page 76 for a complete chart of the rulerships between signs, houses, and planets.

We will now review and deepen our understanding of the planetary signs.

The Planets and Their "Roles"

Inside the ring of zodiac signs you can see other symbols. These are the Sun, the Moon, the planets, and other important points in the heavens. Here are the symbols for those bodies:

THE HEAVENLY BODIES
& THEIR SYMBOLS

Sun	☉
Mercury	☿
Venus	♀
Moon	☽
Mars	♂
Jupiter	♃
Saturn	♄
Uranus	♅
Neptune	♆
Pluto	♇
Chiron	⚷

You can compare the planets to characters in a play. The main characters—the princess, the king, the evil enemy, the hero—come together to act out different stories. How they do that depends on the nature of the play—tragedy or comedy. In astrology, each planet has a specific role to play, superimposed on the particularities of the play. The role of a planet varies according to its placement in the astrological signs that support or hinder their expression.

The planetary principles in astrology are often seen as gods and goddesses, which makes sense because they represent universal laws and patterns.

The Sun, as the life-giving center of our universe, also represents the center of our ego, our self-consciousness, our self-image and identity, personal pride, willpower, how others will perceive us, our overall life force and vitality, and the universal male energy in our life: authority of any kind, the father, or later the partner we will be attracted to. The Sun reflects the part in our persona that we are usually very aware of and identify with. In an archetypical way, you could say the Sun is the king, the ruler of the whole.

The Moon is the universal feminine symbol: the mother, the queen, the giver of life and nourishment, our soul and the unconscious, our emotional makeup, warmth of feelings. The Moon defines how we experience the world through our emotional filter and connects us through her deep well of fantasy to creativity and imagination. She receives through magnetism and passivity.

Mercury was the Roman messenger of the gods. He represents our mind, intellect, the way we think and communicate. Mercury is a teacher and traveler. He loves to explore, discuss, and learn. He is extremely flexible, with a connection between things, but neutral and impartial, like air. He is very curious, sometimes mischievous and playful.

Venus is the Roman goddess of beauty and love. Venus always searches for balance and harmony in all affairs. She shows us how to love, open our hearts, and surround ourselves with beauty. She is the heart longing to surrender, to become one with another. Venus has high ideals and standards. She is sensitive and gentle. This goddess infuses the sexual act with love and sensuality. Her eternal spirit is that of the girl, the princess, the beloved partner. I also would call the qualities we attribute to the heart chakra, like self-love and connectedness, Venusian.

Mars is the warrior, lover, and champion of Venus. He is a god in his own right. He is a courageous fighter who likes to initiate new things. His strong willpower, stamina, and strength aid him in conquering the world. He is single-mindedly committed to his cause, flying straight as an arrow toward his goal. He is direct, uncompromising, honest, and sometimes abrasive. Mars represents our aggression, physical energy, and determination.

Jupiter was also known as Zeus, king of the Greek gods, the deity of the sky. He rules the heavens and the Earth and infuses us with our sense of ethics, morality, and social conscience. He helps us maintain order in our lives through rules and laws. His interest is in philosophy, religion, and the deeper meaning of life. His strengths are the ability to synthesize and a sense of oneness and equality. Everything about Jupiter is expansive. In the old astrology, he was called the bringer of fortune because of his ability to show us where we will find meaning and fulfillment in our life.

Saturn appears in both Greek and Roman mythology as Kronos. He was the father of Zeus. As a Roman God, he was thought of as the ruler of time and was often depicted as an old man with a gray beard.

As a planetary principle, we think of Saturn as the father, reality as it is, old age, the material world, and law and order. Saturn is dispassionate, practical, limiting, restricting, concentrating, and integrating. He also represents focus and fears. He was previously considered a harsh deity and was seen as a more unfortunate symbol in the chart. Saturn challenges us to look deep inside ourselves and examine our fears and restrictions. In that sense, he shines the light of consciousness into the dark.

Uranus is an outer planet (beyond Saturn) that was first discovered 1781 and therefore does not appear in mythology. Astrologers today see him as the prototype of the visionary and rebel. He is thought of as getting the upper hand on authority figures, fighting for good and the underprivileged, for equality and freedom. He represents the ideal of change for the better.

Uranus represents intuition, inspiration, ingenuity, science, and creative intelligence springing up from the well of universal intelligence and consciousness. He is recognized in sudden lightning speed, the principle of change, rhythms, and the transcendence of finite life. He inspires us to strive for uniqueness and the higher realms of consciousness. He has the inner strength to be different and original, thus becoming a role model, inspiration, and leader for many.

Neptune is another modern-day outer planet, discovered in 1846. He is the god of the sea, the role formerly attributed to the Roman god Poseidon. In astrology Neptune is the god of the higher states of all-encompassing love, agape, higher states of consciousness of oneness and connectedness, and deep compassion and empathy. He transcends the experience of our mundane life into the spiritual realms and reaches into the collective unconscious. He is the mystic saint, the monk who devotes his life to the mysteries, the selfless healer of body and soul, the spiritual adviser. He offers the duality of highest inspiration and insights, but also the flip side of illusions, addictions, paralysis, and feebleness. In our chart he shows us where our deepest longing of the soul is.

Pluto, the god of the underworld, is the last of the modern outer planets. Pluto correlates with the individual and deep collective unconscious. He is called the Phoenix that rises from the ashes because he transforms us through death and rebirth. Pluto is thought of as destruction and transformation in many ways and on many levels. He is our dark side, radical and uncompromising and therefore very uncomfortable for our ego identification, because he forces us into metamorphosis even against our will. His will for power can be very destructive. He is demanding, unyielding, bossy, charismatic, extreme, and very influential in any sphere he sets his mind to.

But Pluto also holds the key to deep rejuvenation and transformation and helps us to reach ever higher levels in our evolution. In the individual chart, he points to the area in our life where we will traverse the most profound change in our identity and self-expression.

Chiron is not one of the ten classical planets used in astrology. Nowadays some astrologers work with many other planetary bodies in addition to the classical ones. I have done my own research on Chiron for many years and have come to appreciate the additional information he provides. Chiron is called the "wounded healer." He shows us where we need to put tremendous effort into healing trauma and early childhood wounds often buried deep in our unconsciousness. It is very challenging and takes great courage to confront those old wounds, but it is indeed necessary for the healing process. At the same time, Chiron opens our heart and lets it flower into deep compassion and empathy for others. He is a spiritual teacher par excellence and gives us the hidden keys to higher levels of consciousness. More in-depth information about Chiron will be found in Chapter 6, along with a list of stones that will directly support Chiron's healing process for you.

Now that we know more about the primary characters in our "play," we return to Melanie's chart.

The planets are placed in the zodiac as they were positioned at the moment of birth. You will notice on Melanie's chart that the planets are not distributed evenly around the ring, but clustered in certain areas. A house that has a planet in it is stronger due to the energy of the planet. Houses with more than one planet are even stronger. The planets add their influence to the characteristics of the house. The influence of a planet on you and your life will be different according to which house it is in. Aries in the Fourth House will have a different impact than would Aries in the Seventh House.

Aspects

Look next at the lines in the middle of the chart. They connect the planets and show the relationships between them. This configuration will look different for each person. Sometimes aspects form distinctive forms like triangles or squares or look like a many-faceted crystal or an arrow pointing toward one planet.

The lines connecting the planets form angles. The angles between those bodies and points, called *aspects*, are very important as they reveal how the planets influence the dynamics in play at the moment of an event. The relative positions of these planets and their interrelationships release particular forces in your life.

On the example charts in this book, aspect lines are labeled with a symbol to indicate their type. Some charts may use colors or a separate table to display this information.

Continuing with our metaphor of characters in a play, the aspects reveal how the characters get along with each other—whether they are on friendly terms, uncomfortable with each other, or locked in struggle.

Some connections are more forceful than others. The most powerful relationships are referred to as "hard" aspects. A hard aspect occurs when two planets are square (□, at a 90-degree angle to each other), in opposition (☍, 180 degrees), or in conjunction (☌, 0 degrees). These are positions of friction that represent challenges related to the principles of the involved planets. They reflect a constant struggle between the characters and point to areas of particular challenge and friction that will reappear thematically throughout your lifetime. Naturally, you will attend to these areas and strive to ease these tensions.

Melanie's chart also includes several "favorable" aspects. These are the trine (△, 120 degrees) and sextile (✶, 60 degrees) lines, which indicate areas of strength and harmony.

Let's review the four basic concepts introduced so far:

- A *planet* is like a character in a play, with its own personality.

- A *sign* is the theme of the play that the characters work with.

- A *house* is the stage on which the play is performed.

- An *aspect* shows how the characters relate to each other.

The Ascendant

The Sun rises at the moment when it appears above the eastern horizon. Signs—because they are constellations and always in apparent movement when viewed from the Earth—rise in the same way, at the moment they appear above the horizon. This could be at any time of the day. The sign that is rising on the eastern horizon at the moment of birth is called the *Ascendant*, or *rising sign*. In Melanie's case, Sagittarius was rising at 2:15 a.m., so Sagittarius is her Ascendant. Your Ascendant represents the potential that you bring into this life and will be able to implement more and more over your lifetime. It will play a major role in shaping your personality, your health, and even, it is believed, your physical appearance.

We say that the Ascendant "rules" the First House. Melanie has two planets in her First House, Saturn and Mars. Saturn and Mars therefore rule Melanie's horoscope overall and are among her most important planets.

The Astrological Signs and Their Meaning

The zodiac symbolizes one cycle (circle) of evolution and growth. As the Earth revolves around the Sun, we all move through one complete cycle of twelve months and the changing seasons. The different characteristics of the astrological signs reflect this cycle of change, corresponding to our personal evolution as we mature step by step.

As the Sun moves through its changing positions in the sky throughout the year (here we are referring of course to the *apparent* movement of the Sun), it passes through the constellations on specific dates. The dates assigned to an astrological sign refer to the dates when the Sun appears to be in that constellation.

Each sign is further assigned to one of the *four elements*: earth, air, fire, or water. And finally, each sign is either *masculine* or *feminine* in its associated qualities.

The table below summarizes the signs with their dates, ruling planets, elements, and gender aspects.

The twelve astrological signs set the themes or script for the planets to play with. The themes can be best explained by looking at characteristics of those born under each particular sign.

1. Aries

On March 21, the Sun enters Aries and is positioned directly above the equator. This marks the Spring Equinox, when the days will grow progressively longer and the nights shorter. Aries is therefore the first sign of the zodiac because it signals the start of a new cycle of light and growth.

TABLE OF ASTROLOGICAL SIGNS

#	Sign	Dates	Ruling Planet	Element	Gender
1	Aries	March 21–April 20	Mars	Fire	Masculine
2	Taurus	April 21–May 21	Venus	Earth	Feminine
3	Gemini	May 22–June 21	Mercury	Air	Masculine
4	Cancer	June 22–July 22	Moon	Water	Feminine
5	Leo	July 23–Aug 22	Sun	Fire	Masculine
6	Virgo	Aug 23–Sept 22	Mercury	Earth	Feminine
7	Libra	Sept 23–Oct 22	Venus	Air	Masculine
8	Scorpio	Oct 23–Nov 22	Pluto	Water	Feminine
9	Sagittarius	Nov 23–Dec 20	Jupiter	Fire	Masculine
10	Capricorn	Dec 21–Jan 19	Saturn	Earth	Feminine
11	Aquarius	Jan 20–Feb 18	Uranus	Air	Masculine
12	Pisces	Feb 19–March 20	Neptune	Water	Feminine

Aries symbolizes all beginnings. Imagine the power of the first blade of grass pushing through the soil toward the light. People who are born at this time of the year have an active, expanding, creative energy flow. People born in Aries are always on the go, courageous, energetic, extroverts, and impulsive. They are leaders, but can also be quite aggressive and domineering. They are individualists, the warriors and pioneers of the zodiac. They like to start projects and set up new movements or companies. Their favorite pastime is creating new things.

2. Taurus

People born under the sign of Taurus are well grounded in reality. They are planners who work toward their goals with deliberate steps, endurance, and patience. They love beautiful things for their inherent value: good food, real estate, land, jewelry, and art. They are loyal to their friends and have a sense of duty that makes them well liked and valued. Because they are ruled by Venus, they have a well-developed aesthetic sense. Combining their appreciation for beauty with their patience and endurance, they make good artists. The Taurus person could also be a farmer, financier, or politician.

3. Gemini

Geminis are very flexible, always interested in new information or subjects, and can converse on practically any topic from their store of knowledge. They have a quick mind and are lively and great communicators. They have the gift of learning easily and can also teach others. They love to read and socialize.

Geminis have an analytical mind: they are always examining their doubts and looking for new angles from which to look at things. They have a tendency to get lost in the details instead of coming to some kind of overview. They dislike boredom and routine and need constant challenges.

A Gemini is like a butterfly moving from flower to flower, engaging in a constant process of learning. They excel in many professions: journalist, writer, teacher, business person, or any of the communication fields.

4. Cancer

Because it is a water sign, Cancer is a very feminine sign. All life on the Earth comes from water. We humans emerged from the oceans. Therefore, Cancer has a powerful life-giving quality. Cancer is the Mother of the zodiac, and home and family are extremely important for Cancer people. They have a deep need for emotional nurturing and holding, which might be provided in a marriage. Their actions are often ruled by their emotional ups and downs. These are very giving people who like to care for and nurture others, whether in their own family or in the caring professions. They also become artists, actors, and musicians.

5. Leo

Leo is a very male fire sign. It represents a strong life force. Leo people are expressive, emotional, extroverted, impulsive, and always expanding their energy. They take calculated risks and are usually very successful in their ventures.

Leo is the king of the zodiac circle. Here the ego is in its strongest expression. The Leo personality is about dominion, being in charge, leading the pack, having everything their way, being admired and served. Of course, a general feeling of entitlement comes with being a king or queen. But on the other hand, Leos have a big heart, are very generous, playful, open, trustworthy, and protective of those who are weaker than they, and they love children.

Leos create their own businesses or take on management positions in large corporations. They need to be independent to feel happy and let their creativity fully flow.

6. Virgo

Virgo people, because they are ruled by Mercury, have a tendency to collect both things and thoughts! Virgos are typical pack rats, with a garage full of accumulated items that they "might use some day." But mentally, they are nonetheless quite organized. They love to analyze and think things through down to the smallest details. Those traits make them good jewelers, accountants, dentists, lawyers, doctors, and scientists. Often, they are very interested in health themes and open to trying different diets throughout their lives.

Virgos are practical, down to earth, investigative, supportive, and helpful. You can often recognize Virgos by their clothing—they tend to prefer small patterns.

7. Libra

Libras value relationships, love, and harmony very highly. They tend to try to please others while neglecting their own needs. They have a gift for sensing and understanding others that makes them skilled psychologists, both professionally and in their relationships. They have a deep longing to create harmony and balance, making them good mediators. At the same time, they have some difficulty with decision making because they are able to see both sides of problems equally.

Libras are charming and entertaining. They have a strong aesthetic sense and love art, style, and beauty in any form.

8. Scorpio

Scorpio is a sign of extremes and opposite polarities. For Scorpios, things are either black or white, never gray.

Scorpios are very deep and complex people, although their depth and intensity can have a dark side that gets them into trouble. It may be difficult to be in a relationship with a Scorpio because they can be rigid and uncompromising. That quality serves them well when they are pursuing goals, because nothing deters them from their objectives. Again, though, they can become obsessive and fixated on ideals in their pursuit of perfection. Scorpios are brilliant and gifted people who make a lasting impression.

At their best, Scorpios are highly successful people. They have the gift of leadership, but they use their leadership abilities behind the scenes. They gravitate toward many professions, where they stand out for their charisma, power, total engagement, determination, perfectionism, and their ability to sacrifice themselves for the greater vision if need be.

9. Sagittarius

As the Sun passes through the stormy depths of Scorpio, things go more smoothly in Sagittarius. Sagittarians are good-hearted, generous, open, independent, active, sociable, and lively companions. They love philosophy, religion, sometimes politics, nature, animals, and world travel.

Sagittarians live large, expansive, successful lives. They are constantly bringing new ideas into the world. They balance their precise, deep thinking with strong intuition and a search for wisdom in the way they live. While Geminis get lost in details, Sagittarians have the ability to assemble the small pieces into a bigger picture that makes sense. They have high ideals and think deeply about the state of the world, which makes them good politicians, diplomats, ministers, missionaries, teachers, and doctors. They require a high degree of independence and initiative in their work.

10. Capricorn

Capricorn begins the last quarter of the zodiac circle and represents a stage of evolution in which social responsibility emerges. Capricorns are not withdrawn; they put themselves into the public eye and success, power, and prestige are important to them. But they hold rigidly to tradition, norms, and rules and are sensitive to what other people think of them. They can cling stubbornly to their notions of right and wrong.

Capricorns are very organized, reality oriented, disciplined, ambitious, patient, and intelligent. They are prepared to invest all effort necessary to reach their goals. They measure themselves and others by performance and success. Loving structured hierarchies, they are the quintessential organizers and bureaucrats—corporate CEOs, government officials, and military officers.

11. Aquarius

The revolutionary thinking of Aquarians counterbalances the rules and order of Capricorn and Leo. Aquarians are highly colorful, original, inventive people who are full of new ideas for making the world a better place. They seek out people to join them in that quest. They are highly nonconformist, independent, and idealistic, always questioning norms and rules. They apply those qualities to assisting weaker members of society. Because Aquarians are always seeking what is new, they have many sudden interruptions, changes, and innovations in their lives. Life is never dull with an Aquarian!

The inventive mind of the Aquarian is put to great use on the frontiers of science, where they go beyond the known and search for new horizons. The inventiveness of Aquarians spans both the technical and the artistic realms. They make excellent researchers, pilots, inventors, composers, actors, painters, and scientists.

12. Pisces

Pisces is the last sign of the zodiac, the sign of conclusion. Each sign encompasses new learning. Much has been integrated in Pisces. Pisceans are full of insights and hence the most compassionate of all the signs. Because they have experienced so much, they have deep empathy and love for others. Pisceans are highly spiritual people. They have a strong sense of connectedness and oneness with the universe. They seek to transcend the material world and connect with the nonphysical realms. They long for higher states of consciousness—which sometimes leads them into trouble with drugs and alcohol.

Pisceans also have a rich inner life filled with fantasies, dreams, and romantic ideas that draws them to express themselves through the creative arts. Pisceans are often mystics, spiritual teachers, monks, or spiritual researchers. Because of their sensitivity to suffering, they often choose to become helpers, healers, doctors, or nurses.

Because Pisceans are not much invested in a strong ego at this twelfth stage of evolution, they have somewhat loose boundaries. They tend to dissolve into their relationship or profession. They have difficulty setting boundaries in relationships and would rather drift away from conflict than confront it head on. The Piscean has the most sensitive and gentle soul of all.

4

How to Read a Birth Chart

A Basic Interpretation of Melanie's Birth Chart

Now that you have been introduced to all of the components of an astrological chart, it's time to see how those elements come together so we can interpret a chart. Reading a chart is an intriguing art, and I think you will enjoy it.

A chart is like a holographic photo: it has fascinating depth and changes as you look at it from different angles. The same chart may yield slightly different interpretations, depending on the state of consciousness (depth of wisdom and knowledge) and creativity of the reader. The object is to obtain the most profound and meaningful reading possible.

A reading progresses in layers, as the different qualities of the chart are laid one upon the other, until a complex picture of the forces at play in the person's makeup and life is reached. This may seem complicated initially, but in the end you will grasp this rich tapestry.

The Structure of a Reading

Here is the structure that guides me through reading a horoscope:

- First I notice how the **four elements** of fire, water, air, and earth are represented in the chart. That gives me a general idea of how the person's individual life themes and personality traits will be expressed through those elemental tendencies. (In-depth information about the elements will be given in Chapter 9.)

- Second, I look at the Rising Sign or **Ascendant** and note if it has any additional planets in it.

- Third, I analyze the **Moon** and the **Sun** in their signs, house positions, and network of aspects.

- I then apply the same analysis to **each planet** in its sign, house, and aspects.

- At the very end I analyze the **Moon Node** as the focal point of learning, karmic destination, and achievement of the soul.

Now let's apply this five-step process to Melanie's chart.

The Four Elements

Melanie is relatively balanced in all four elements, which means she can express herself through all of their virtues and vices. But the number of planets in Aquarius shows that she leans a little toward **air**. This tells me that in general she is a very flexible, versatile, curious woman who is easily bored and needs a constant variety of mental challenges and inspiration. Melanie filters the world mainly through her mind and loves contact with people and communication. Her basic makeup is a nice base for a reading—she will be open to learning about all the new concepts that will be presented.

Ascendant

Each sign and each planet is associated with specific characteristics. Melanie's Ascendant, **Sagittarius**, represents the element fire and the principle of expansion, or overcoming limitations and boundaries. Melanie is therefore someone who constantly looks for deeper meaning in life. She seeks philosophical understanding, a sense of the bigger picture. She is both energetic and enigmatic in her self-expression.

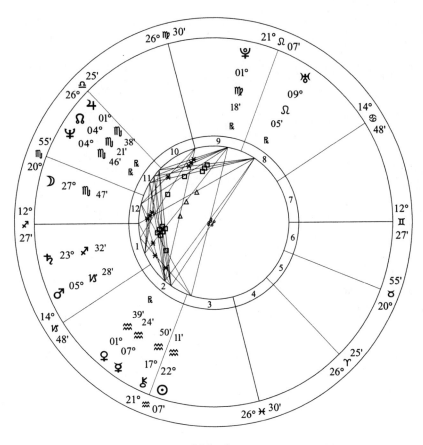

Melanie
February 11, 1958 / 2:15 a.m. / Newport Beach, California

In Melanie's **First House** we see **Saturn in Sagittarius** and **Mars in Capricorn**.

Saturn shows us our limitations and fears and challenges us to grow wherever he stands in the chart. People with Saturn in the First House are usually very grounded, serious, and well organized, and usually must expend extra effort to reach their goals. But it is as if some invisible curtain separates the "Saturnine" person from a more light-hearted approach to life. Saturn lends depth and sincerity to Melanie's philosophical understanding and values. She has a need to inquire into who she is as a person and her spiritual soul.

Mars as the second male principle shows us how our physical energy flows. As much as Saturn might be experienced as an initial roadblock, Mars is the engine that gets the show on the road. Mars in Capricorn gives Melanie the ability to focus her strength, and empowers her with energy in her self-expression so that she will stand out—the moment she enters a room, people will notice. As her life unfolds, Melanie will have to find a safe way to deal with the flip side of Mars in this position and learn how to express her anger and aggression. With Mars in the First House, a person is either quick to show aggression or easily victimized by other aggressors.

Moon and Sun

In Melanie's chart, at the moment of her birth, the **Moon** was located in the **Twelfth House** in the sign of **Scorpio**. This gives us specific information about Melanie's emotional makeup: her perceptions of the world and how she acts in the world stirred by her emotions.

The Moon represents the principles of nurturing, mother, giving life, receiving and giving, and our unconscious mind. It represents in general how we feel about life and what we need to feel safe. Scorpio is a sign of extremes and opposite polarities. It encompasses the depths of the soul, including its darkest aspects. Scorpios are complex and charismatic people, perfectionists, at times uncompromising, sharply intellectual and gifted, and determined in pursuing goals.

Melanie's Moon positioned in Scorpio tells us she is a person of great emotional depth. She does not always show her own feelings, but she is very good at tuning into other people's feelings and needs. She is always striving to be her best self and in a constant process of learning about herself.

The Twelfth House is overlaid by the twelfth sign, **Pisces**, so to understand Melanie's Moon, we need to add the qualities of Pisces. This tells us that she is very compassionate and empathic and loves to help and nurture others. Her longing to be of service expresses itself in her chosen profession as a psychotherapist.

Now we look at the different **aspects** that the **Moon** might have to other planets. We look especially for the hard aspects that show the challenges and frictions between the different parts of Melanie's personality. Her Moon has a **square** to her **Sun** and also to **Pluto.** This means that there is tension between how Melanie feels in the world, her deep, intense, compassionate, and loving nature (Scorpio/Pisces) and the way she presents herself to the outside (through her Sun). The square with Pluto emphasizes the depth of her feelings and a certain rigidity in her tendency to see things as black and white, and will strengthen the Scorpio influence on her emotional makeup. Pluto is the ruler of Scorpio, so there is a double influence on Melanie's Moon, which represents feelings and the unconscious mind.

Melanie's **Sun** is in **Aquarius**, revealing that she is open minded, interested in new things, and a visionary. These qualities manifest in her professional life, where she is very unorthodox and at the forefront of research into new methods of psychotherapy. Her Sun in the **Third House** adds the mental flexibility of Gemini and a love for teaching, writing, and counseling. **The Pluto opposition** to her Sun adds depth and commitment and her striving for changing her self-perception. Throughout her lifetime Melanie will be seeking to transform and perfect herself. She could also become very well known if she chooses.

Planets in Their Signs, Houses, and Aspects

To understand your birth chart, you next look at the position of each planet in the signs and the houses.

Melanie's **Mercury** is also in **Aquarius**, which informs us about her way of thinking and communicating. Hers is a very innovative and flexible mind, inquiring and curious. Mercury is also in the **Second House**, indicating an overlay of Taurus. Taurus is an earth sign with a propensity for very concrete and solid things, not as erratic and sudden as the **Uranus opposition** to this Mercury might suggest. So there is some friction between Melanie's free-flowing thinking, intuitive knowledge, and spontaneous inspirations and the safety of what is familiar, historical, and tangible.

She also has her Sun in Aquarius, which leads me to think that she will lean toward the innovative and inspirational side of this duality. In that case, the Taurus side might help her to manifest her thoughts in some concrete and substantial way, such as writing a book or dissertation or doing research.

Also, **Neptune** is **squaring** her **Mercury**, which will appear as a highly sensitive and finely tuned mind. With a square and an opposition of both outer planets—Uranus and Neptune, which connect us to the collective unconscious and are highly inspiring—she is exceptionally quick and intuitive in her thought processes. She may even possess psychic abilities.

Melanie's **Venus** is also in **Aquarius**. This goddess of love, arts, and harmony has a rather extreme sense of aesthetics and, in fact, tends to push the envelope in many ways. In art and aesthetics, she will prefer bold colors, possibly abstract art, and unusual combinations. She might even express herself artistically in some way, which would go well with her Venus position in the **Second House** ruled by **Taurus**. As an artist, she is very independent and more likely to create a new trend than follow one.

In real life, Melanie loves jewelry and even creates her own wonderful beaded pieces to grace herself. She is interested in art and is married to a painter.

In the relationship arena, Melanie is unconventional and autonomous. Being in the Second House, this Venus might get married, but she and her spouse might live in separate apartments in the same building to preserve her independence. Or she might be the bread winner while her husband takes care of the children—remember that she is unconventional, an innovator, and in a process of constant change. In addition, her **Uranus opposition** will further strengthen her individuality and willingness to stand out and be different from the people around her.

Jupiter shows us where we can find fulfillment and joy as we align ourselves with deeper meaning and the longing of our soul. Melanie's

Jupiter is in **Scorpio** and in the **Eleventh House**, which is ruled by **Aquarius.** Melanie's joy and satisfaction come from her impetus to keep growing and changing in profound ways. Her search for her spiritual roots is of utmost importance to her.

At this point, you are beginning to see how the interplay of many forces in the horoscope comes together to create an individual's complex personality and life course. The salient features at work in Melanie's chart are the transformational energy of Scorpio and Pluto, as well as her four planets in Aquarius.

The **square aspects** of **Jupiter** to **Uranus** and **Mercury** add some friction through sudden changes and the attempt to understand things intellectually, which is really impossible to do all of the time. In spirituality, what really counts for the soul is a profound experience of the divine, not merely reading about it. An intellectual investigation of spirituality might satisfy our curiosity, but in the end what really matters is the undeniable experience of God and the mystery of life.

Now let's turn to Melanie's **Chiron** in **Aquarius,** in the **Second House,** in **conjunction** with the **Sun, opposition** to **Uranus.**

Chiron—the wounded healer—shows us where we have been traumatized and hurt, and therefore need to heal and grow. With Chiron being so close to and merging with the energies of the Sun, it is certain that the strong, at times even outrageous, qualities of Aquarius will always be clamoring for expression in Melanie's life. This may well create difficulties for Melanie. She might have had a strong, controlling father or other authority figure in her early life, or perhaps she has come from a very conventional family with oppressive belief systems that she has had to transcend. The Pluto opposition to her Sun/Chiron conjunction points to a long road of transformation as Melanie works to establish her individuality and grow into the unique, highly unconventional person she is meant to be.

This polarity between Melanie's unfettered, creative side and the more restrained elements present in her personality and her environment was a central focus of my reading. When this duality was brought into the light of consciousness, Melanie readily recognized the presence of opposing forces within her. She appeared deeply relaxed after making peace with those forces for the first time in her life.

And that is the power of astrology: by making new connections, giving a name to seemingly opposite forces in the personality, we can make peace with ourselves through deep acceptance of what is.

I mentioned earlier that the more planets there are in one sign, the more important that sign is and the more visible its themes become in our lives. In Melanie's chart, four planetary bodies out of eleven are in Aquarius, so it is clear that Aquarius plays a major role in her life. There is no way to get around this influence of Aquarius!

Moon Node

At the end of a reading, looking at the **Moon Node** (☊) often helps to tie everything together and understand the general direction of the chart. Melanie's Moon Node is in **Scorpio** in the **Eleventh House**. That means that all of the Scorpio, Aquarius, and Pluto themes discussed above pose a significant challenge for her.

A compassionate and nonjudgmental discussion of this challenge was the way to deepen Melanie's understanding of the difficulties in her life and help her to find peace with her Scorpio energies. Pluto and Scorpio themes sometimes lead to a tendency to become victimized and to then project those dark energies onto the people and surrounding world, making a compassionate reading all the more important.

Because her Moon Node is in Scorpio, I focused on Melanie's tendency to split off negative traits, to suppress and deny them as part of herself. It is never healthy to deny parts of the self. Instead, we must make peace with them or find constructive ways to express them. Suppressed parts of the self manifest as negativity, destruction, self criticism, obsessive behavior, and hatefulness towards one self and others.

Again and again during my many years of giving astrological readings, I have had to make people aware of the deep Plutonic forces within them. People are almost always relieved and grateful to finally understand these forces and the difficult events that have been perplexing them. When we shine the light of awareness on a formerly dark and misunderstood corner of the self, we lose our fear of that element and no longer feel overwhelmed by it. In astrology, truth is what sets us free.

Now you have an example of how all these layers of planets, signs, houses, and aspects create a template for your personality and your life as depicted on your birth chart. Knowledge is power! In Chapter 6 we will use this understanding to identify healing gemstones that will restore balance to your life and ease areas of friction.

5

Astrology and Gemstones

*Using the Gifts of Mother Earth
for Personal Growth and Healing*

By now you understand the basic astrological principle of "as above so below," which allows us to read the analogue relations among the planets and extrapolate those principles to things here on the Earth: to events in our lives as well as to our natural environment. The universal principles that govern the planets are also seen on the much smaller level of gemstones, crystals, and metals. If you are able to discover the type of balance and support that you need, you can seek those properties in specific gemstones and use stones in your healing process.

Let's take the example of Hematite to illustrate. The chemical composition of Hematite is Fe_2O_3, or iron oxide. It is a silvery gray metallic to black opaque stone that bleeds red into the water when cut and polished. We learned previously that the color red and iron are associated with Mars, the red planet. Mars is the warrior and conqueror and represents our male, physical and sexual energy, our life force, our aggression, impulses, will, discernment, and courage. So Hematite will be helpful for all Mars-related matters and can help strengthen our life force, balance aggression and sexual energy, and assist us with our will, courage, and discernment. If you are in a time in your life where you feel a lot of fatigue, feel listless and without initiative or direction, it might be a good idea to support yourself with a gemstone with Mars qualities to realign your energy flow.

Every internal or physical process you find yourself in is represented by some astrological planetary configuration. Understanding the planetary representation gives you the conscious choice of how you want that principle to play out in your life and how gemstones can support those processes.

Gemstones Radiate Healing Energy

All matter is energy in one form or another. That energy is emitted in the form of waves that vibrate at a certain frequency. Because nature has created gemstones with a very specific and balanced crystal structure, they are perfect, harmonious compositions that radiate balanced energy into our system. We know this intuitively and thus we are drawn to them for their healing and balancing properties. Most people are able to sense this radiation of energy. They might say, "This is such a beautiful stone!" and be drawn to it because of the positive energy they feel.

Gemstones also radiate colored light frequencies into our own energy field. Their translucent quality is a bridge between the material and the spiritual realms. Because gemstones represent the highest form of radiant light frequencies in physical matter, they are able to help us integrate our highest potential.

The Complex Signature of Gemstones

Almost every woman knows her birthstone. Actually, I believe that birthstones as we know them were a marketing invention of the jewelry business. But birthstones are also an expression of our intuitive knowledge of the healing and transcending qualities of gemstones and our longing to touch the mystery of life.

There are twelve birthstones associated with the signs of the zodiac. The list of specific stones has varied throughout history, but jewelers have adopted an official list—which may not actually be based on true astrological principles. The birthstones that most people are familiar with are based on the position of the Sun in the zodiac in the birth month. This is a good start, but it may well be insufficient to simply know your birth month, because your birth chart is a complex representation of many different planetary factors. In order to identify the stone that will have a distinct impact on your unique soul, it is important to study your birth chart in all its complexity.

Each gemstone enfolds a specific assemblage of different planetary principles. This is called the "signature" of the stone. The signature gives each gemstone a very different individual "personality" that makes it unique.

Let's look at an example. The Diamond, our most expensive and cherished gemstone, occurs in all colors, including colorless, yellow, brown, green, blue, reddish, and black. It holds qualities of Mars, Venus, the Sun, Saturn, or Uranus depending on its color.

Diamond is the hardest of all stones and therefore tops the Mohs' hardness scale[1] with a hardness of 10. This makes it a Saturn stone, because Saturn represents the principles of crystallization, hardness, and contraction. At the same time, Diamond has the highest brilliancy and reflection of all gems, which clearly makes it a Sun stone.

The chemical composition of Diamond is crystallized carbon, which is again Saturn. The crystal structure is mainly octahedrons or a double pyramid, which makes it both Mars and Venus. Mars is reflected in the "pointedness" of the pyramid structure, reminiscent of a sword. The double pyramid is a very balanced form mirrored around the midline, in keeping with the balance and harmony of Venus.

To give an example of the relevance of color, a blue Diamond is associated with Uranus, because in fact Uranus is blue.

....

1 In 1822, the German mineralogist Friedrich Mohs devised the Mohs Hardness Scale, a simple method of rating the hardness of minerals on a scale of 1 to 10 by comparing their resistance to scratching. Gemstones used for jewelry need to have a scratch resistance of 6 or more. Diamond is the hardest mineral, with a scratch resistance of 10. Other examples of gemstones with suitable hardness for jewelry include Corundum (Rubies and Sapphires, 9), Topaz (8), Quartz (including Amethyst and Citrine, 7) and Feldspar (6).

How can we use this information to our best advantage?

The signature of a gemstone tells us which principles the stone is beneficial for. For example, a Saturn/Sun conjunction in Libra or Aries points to a challenge surrounding the conflicting principles of constriction versus life force. The Diamond, whose signature incorporates both Saturn and Sun principles, would be the perfect stone to smooth out this conflict. Bringing Diamond into your energy field can balance those conflicting forces within yourself. For example, the Diamond could enhance and focus your creative self-expression in your personal and professional life. It could help you get started on new projects and align your energy with your intention.

With the diagnostic help of the signatures of gemstones, we are equipped to select exactly the right stone that is needed in each moment of our lives. The planetary associations of common gemstones are charted on pages 89–92 and listed in the profiles in Chapter 7.

Identifying Your Main Life Themes

Your birth chart offers you a fascinating view of the thematic challenges and trials that may recur throughout your life. These are the areas you need to work on most, searching for ever more evolved ways of dealing with those themes.

It is important to come to an understanding of the principles underlying our challenges. For example, difficulty with authority figures reflects, in essence, a struggle to grow into one's own strength and power. This is an evolutionary struggle faced by everyone, not only by rebellious teenagers! With this insight, we are empowered to step out of the victim position and take responsibility for ourselves. When we quietly accept our personal power and responsibility to exercise it, the conflict with authority falls away.

We may use astrological principles to identify potential friction between planets according to their position in the signs and houses. That friction is expressed as conflicts among specific principles in your life. In Chapter 6, we'll work on identifying these main conflict themes, which will enable you to choose gemstones whose signatures will help to balance those conflicts.

Moving through Transits with the Help of Gemstones

From the moment of our birth, represented by the birth chart, the planets continue moving through their positions in the zodiac. Their movement across the heavens is referred to as a "transit." When a planet stands at a specific angle relative to its original position in the birth chart, it will come into influence in your life. Studying these transit aspects reveals the planetary forces in effect at a specific time in your life. It can alert you to both opportunities and challenges that may arise during a particular period and may help you to understand times when things seem particularly difficult.

Often, people turn to an astrologer for a reading when they feel like they are in a difficult time in their life and they want to get a deeper understanding of what is fueling those challenges. I often find in these cases that there is a difficult transit taking place, usually with the outer planets, especially Saturn.

You can find the current position and aspects of the planets in any astrological calendar or datebook to determine if you are experiencing a difficult transit. While the Moon transits through a sign every two or three days, the other planets transit more slowly.

With a new and deeper perspective on the dynamics at work in your life at present, you are better equipped to make conscious choices and decisions. You can support those intentions by choosing a gemstone that has exactly the right signature for the moment.

For example, you may be experiencing difficulties due to a Saturn transit over the Sun—shown by a conjunction or another hard aspect. Because the Diamond incorporates the principles of both Saturn and the Sun, it can balance and ease that transit. It's time to get out your Diamond ring! This transit may offer an opportunity for new growth as you traverse this difficult period: a chance to deepen your self-understanding about your personality, creative potential, and self-expression (all Sun principles), while finding new ways to achieve clarity about your limiting fears and personality traits (Saturn principles).

The above example shows that although a planetary configuration may appear to be problematic on the surface and may indeed bring on a period of difficulty, the right understanding can help you combine the best qualities of each planet to resolve and move beyond difficulties—supported by the right gemstone.

Transits of Saturn and the outer planets—Uranus, Neptune, and Pluto—are often fraught with difficulty. You will want to consider using Opal to ease these periods.

Opal does not have a crystal structure—its molecules are arranged in layers consisting of tiny spheres of silica that create an ever-changing rainbow of reflected light. These qualities of change and movement make Opals the most wonderful allies for times and processes of transformation and growth.

Each Stone has its Own Personality

We have seen that each gemstone has a signature that reveals its qualities and the impact it can have on you. But in my experience, there is more to it than that: not only does each type of gemstone have its characteristic qualities, but each individual specimen of a stone has its own distinct appearance and personality. So, for example, you must choose not only *an* Opal, but *the* Opal that is just right for you.

The Opals constitute a beautiful and rich family of stones characterized by a variety of intense color combinations and "opalescence," which is a rainbowlike sparkling and iridescence that changes the stone's colors when viewed from different angles. As you begin to look at Opals to support you in your process of growth and transformation, you will quickly realize that there is a whole world of different and enchanting Opals. Each gemstone of any type is a unique individual, but this is especially true in the world of the beautiful Opals—there are simply no two Opals alike. If you fall in love with one while you are out shopping, it is best to buy it right away because you will never find the same stone again.

Tuning into your intuition will help you to find the stone that is the most balancing for you. I usually advise choosing the stone that appeals to you the most, the one that you find most beautiful and enchanting. A gemstone's beauty is the language it uses to reach out to you and communicate with you. There are other ways to determine which exact gemstone is the most beneficial for you, but the language of beauty is the simplest.

Using Kinesiology to Find the Right Gemstone

Another way to find the one particular stone that is the most power-ful gem for you is to use kinesiology. Kinesiology is a process that tests muscle response (by manually pushing against the muscle) in order to understand how the body, mind, spirit, and environment work to-gether. Kinesiology is like tapping into a universal computer bank that will give you a simple yes or no answer to any question you ask. Be-cause of that, it is being used increasingly in many healing professions as a very noninvasive diagnostic tool. I myself have had body workers, chiropractors, a dentist, and a homeopath use it on me to find the right remedy, material, or treatment approach.

You can easily apply kinesiology yourself. For example, you might want to test a specific medication or food to find out whether it agrees with you and balances your system. To do this, you first test your nor-mal arm strength: While standing, lift one arm straight out to your side and have someone push it back down, noting your muscle resistance. Then hold the object you want to test to your chest with one hand while your partner pushes down your outstretched opposite arm. You may well notice a significant difference among different objects that you test. You might be surprised to find that you are unable to resist the downward pressure on your arm even when you try with all your might. The object that yields that result is definitely not supportive of your system!

You can have fun with kinesiology testing a variety of foods, sugar, medications, and of course gemstones, noting whether those seem to support or weaken your system.

As we learned above, each stone is an individual. Three Rubies simi-lar in size and color might have very different individual frequencies, possibly relating to where they were mined. There might be slight dif-ferences in the chemical composition as well. Those differences will not be apparent to the eye, but you can use kinesiology to discover which stone most clearly strengthens you. With kinesiology you might be surprised to learn that even a tiny gemstone can have an impact on your system.

So, first look for the beauty of a gemstone. Find one that speaks to your heart. If you feel unsure about your choice, test it with kinesiology.

Intuition and the Magic of Beauty

I believe that there is a place of wisdom and intuition inside each of us, and that when we are able to go to that place, we are guided by truth and love. In that place, we discover what path to walk and which choices to make.

The experience and appreciation of beauty is a uniquely human quality. I have never heard a dog complain about his dog house being ugly! We are able to cherish beauty for its intrinsic value whether or not there is monetary value attached to it. (Expensive things always seem to appeal to me!) When our instinctual and physical needs are taken care of, the soul longs for nourishment beyond that. Beauty is food for the soul!

Beauty is a celebration of life in all its potential, a bridge to the unfolding mystery of life. Who is not touched by the Sun setting over the ocean, the stars sparkling on a cloudless night, or a work of art like Michelangelo's statue of David? Our soul guides us toward beauty and its enfolding in our life, bringing us into the here and now with our awareness of its presence.

In gemstone and crystal jewelry, magic and beauty created by nature are enhanced by human creativity to delight, energize, and heal us.

Jewelry is one of our most intimate possessions: it is worn on the body and becomes part of us physically and energetically. At every moment of the day, we can have the pleasure of looking at our ring with its beautiful specimen. So jewelry is first of all a gift for our soul to enjoy and cherish. But beyond that, jewelry tells the world who we are and what our values are.

Beauty is a luxury not only because it is sometimes expensive, as in the case of art objects or jewelry, but because a longing for it arises in the heart once our basic physical survival needs are met.

When you are searching for a piece of jewelry, just trust your heart and you will find your most healing and uplifting gem.

Wedding Bands and Heart-Opening Stones

A wedding band is a circle with no beginning and no end, a symbol of eternity. The circle symbolizes a couple's commitment and intention to be together always in a bond of marital love.

Generally we feel attracted to people who complement us, who represent aspects that are latent in ourselves. By being with someone who is living the qualities that we lack or have not yet discovered, we can learn about those qualities. In a man's chart, Venus and the Moon represent the feminine aspect that he would like to integrate into his own personality. For a woman, the Sun and Mars position represent the male principle.

So, in general, it is beneficial for a couple to wear stones that represent the male and female principles that they would like to integrate with each other. For example, a man might wish to wear a Moonstone, because the Moonstone represents the Moon and opens up the connection to the unconscious, the feminine, intuition, and creative potential. When Venus or the Moon are in conjunction with Saturn, Pluto, Uranus, or Neptune (the "hard" planets), you might expect challenges or friction and will need to seek a gemstone with just the right signature to counteract those forces.

For a woman, wearing stones with the right signature for her Sun and Mars will help her to integrate the masculine principles. That might mean a balance in her assertiveness, creative expression, her physical and sexual energy, aggression, and personal will.

The heart-opening stones are wonderful to wear in a wedding band. I often recommend the Ruby for wedding bands. Ruby is the second hardest stone on the Mohs' hardness scale, which makes it a very durable stone and excellent for wedding bands. Ruby is also the stone of unconditional love and helps us to develop the potentials of the heart.

The Rubellite Tourmaline is also a beautiful heart-opening stone. Rubellite symbolizes unconditional love and teaches us self-love. It has a hardness of 7–7½, which is sufficient for a ring.

The Sapphire belongs to the Corundum family, like the Ruby. It is as hard and durable as the Ruby. Sapphires occur in a great many colors, including blue, yellow, pink, and orange. They symbolize different aspects of our enfoldment (the unfolding of the soul toward its highest potential) and make a wonderful companion on that journey.

The Diamond is one of the most beautiful stones of all. As we learned earlier, it has the highest reflection of light and is the hardest and most durable of all gems. The Diamond represents the life force of the Sun, the highest expression of light and consciousness in our solar system.

The Opal is the stone of the mystic, shaman, artist, and healer in us. It is a wonderful companion for a marriage consciously based on spiritual principles. It is a stone for support during times of transformation and intense change. The Opal needs to be handled with care. It is not a very durable stone and sensitive to chemicals, knocks, and pressure. If you choose an Opal as an ally for your mutual process of growing together, you have to expect to exchange your stones once in a while. In my wedding band, I have an Opal as a center stone with a Ruby and a Diamond as accent stones; I am wearing my second Opal in ten years of marriage.

Healing Through Transformation and Integration of Insights

We all have had the experience, both in our own lives and through observing others, of a challenge turning out to be to our benefit. As we work through problems, we become more and more skilled at the art of living. If we look at problems through astrological glasses, we can determine the universal principles underlying them and have more choices for solving them. As we integrate those insights, we become better equipped to act.

For example, you might have a Neptune/Sun conjunction in the Twelfth House in your chart. That might manifest in a problematic way as an addiction to alcohol or drugs. The underlying universal principle here is Neptune—a desire to transcend into nonconceptual realms beyond our ego nature, where we experience things directly, beyond our usual perceptions and thoughts. The Sun represents our self-identification, our personality, how we act in our life. The Neptune/Sun theme is about transcending our limited ego structure, of who we think we are. It is about expanding into higher states of consciousness; transforming a weak ego structure into a sense of connectedness with the divine, finding a spiritual meaning in life, being of service for the greater good, serving something or someone beyond our own personal gain or ego satisfaction.

Drugs and alcohol are ways that some people try to escape from the ordinary state of consciousness into something larger beyond their normal perception of the world. This is true of both drug addicts and people who use drugs to enhance religious experience or creativity: both are seeking to escape the ego structure and ordinary experience. A deep longing of the soul for a sense of connectedness and belonging often drives this choice.

Reaching a higher state of consciousness is indeed a positive goal, but given the dangers of alcohol and drugs, an alternative way to live the Neptune/Sun principle would be to consciously choose a lifestyle guided by spirituality, finding ways to experience ourselves as a part of the divine. One way to fill that yearning of the soul would be to meditate on a daily basis. There are many spiritual paths that one could choose to walk, leading to connectedness with the divine, faith, and trust.

To support that process of transcending our ordinary state of consciousness, we could use Amethyst. Amethyst would help to connect us with our spiritual nature, to discover that we are spiritual beings having a human experience, not the other way around. *Amethyst* comes from a Greek word meaning "remedy against drunkenness." When we access higher planes of consciousness, where we feel ourselves held, comforted, and nourished by the divine, our longing for the anesthetizing effect of substances such as alcohol and drugs slowly dissipates.

We could also choose an Opal in combination with an Amethyst. Opal is a healer and mentor during times of transition and intensive change. Opal helps to change limiting beliefs and mental patterns. It connects us to the collective unconscious and all the treasures it enfolds. It fuels our intuition with sudden sparks of insight and wisdom. The combinations of these two wonderful stones can be a constant reminder of that journey in addition to the harmonizing frequency of these gems in our energy field.

So you can see that each principle underlying a period of challenge can be expressed in either a positive or a negative fashion. Consciousness is the key to finding the positive path, because consciousness makes you aware of choices.

Finding Meaning and Focus in Life

Many people have made incredible achievements in their lives by reframing their challenges and problems in order to think about them in a new way. For example, many people express that their cancer or other life-threatening illness has been the biggest gift in their life.

The mind is incredibly strong. We can make our mind our ally by using it to consciously focus on a new meaning in a situation in a way that serves us best. This is called "reframing" in hypnotherapy and Neurolinguistic Programming (NLP). Hypnotherapy and NLP work by changing the patterns and beliefs programmed into our mind by all our accumulated experiences throughout our lives. Reframing is accomplished by changing the context or representation of a problem in order to resolve a conflict.

We have the power to reframe any event in our life by asking ourselves the question, what could be the gift in this for me? How else could I look at this situation? What else could this mean for me? For example, I might get upset because I just cleaned the kitchen floor and then my children and husband come through and leave footprints everywhere—or I can choose to see my family's footprints as an expression of a happy family living together. Which perspective will better serve me?

When we use gemstones for healing and support, we are also choosing a higher perspective and sometimes reframing or giving new meaning to a situation. When we are aware of the metaphysical properties of a gemstone, we can choose to adopt that perspective consciously. For example, you might choose to wear a Ruby, the stone of unconditional love and positive self-expression. When you feel distressed or insecure you can look at the Ruby and ask, what would Love do? Over time, as you absorb Ruby's message of love, you will find yourself feeling calmer and more secure and responding to stressful situations with more serenity.

Life just works better and feels better when we live it from a meaningful and loving point of view. When we make beautiful and meaningful gems a part of our life, we choose beauty and harmony over stress and friction.

Anchoring: Using the Unconscious Mind

An important technique in neurolinguistic programming (NLP) is referred to as "anchoring." This is a process in which you consciously choose a focal point and your unconscious mind automatically connects that focus with a chosen response. In my work I like to apply this mechanism by talking to my clients about the metaphysical properties of gemstones. This is a way of programming the information into the unconscious mind for later retrieval.

Anchoring can operate in any representational system: sight, sound, feeling, smell, or taste. We are anchoring ourselves all the time. You may have heard a song ten years ago when you had that first dance with your spouse. It has become your song. You hear it now on the radio as you drive down the road, and it brings up all the feelings you had all those years ago, dancing with the one you were to fall in love with. Or you might be at the mall and you smell a fragrance that you recognize right away: it is just how your grandmother used to smell, and for a moment it will bring back all the feelings and the connection you felt with your grandmother.

In NLP, anchoring is used to create a desired resourceful state and sometimes to override negative imprints we have. It is possible to anchor a state of confidence and balance by remembering a time when you were having an experience of those qualities. When you are at the peak of that memory and feel what you were feeling at that time, you bring your thumb and forefinger together and press them several times (called "pulsating"). This installs the state in the subconscious. Then you interrupt your state by doing something else. When you put your fingers together again and pulsate them, you will again feel that powerful state of confidence and balance. Imagine that you have a job interview and all you need to do is pulsate your fingers together to achieve a resourceful state.

There are many ways to use this simple but very effective technique to our benefit. I suggest using it with your gemstones and jewelry. If you are given a piece of jewelry by your beloved one for a special occasion—the birth of a child, that special holiday in Hawaii, your anniversary—it will always be connected with that event and the intention and love it was given with. Wearing that piece and looking at it when you are upset or need comfort can have a very harmonizing impact on you.

The same holds true for any conscious connection you are creating with a piece of jewelry. If I am creating a piece of jewelry for someone after she has had a reading of her astrological chart and we have explored the metaphysical connection between her issues and her healing stones, that piece will always be an anchor and unconscious reminder of the information received during the reading.

Anchoring taps into the power of our own thoughts to heal and support us. Through anchoring, a gemstone can induce a state of "unconscious mindfulness" that reminds us to strive for the qualities that the stone supports. For example, if I know that Opal is the stone to help me through difficult times of change and transformation, that is exactly what the Opal I am wearing on my body will do for me.

I find anchoring to be a very elegant way to use the ability of the mind to work for us in our best interest.

During my thirty years of experience with jewelry and gemstones, I have come to know that there are two levels of healing impact. One is the signature and frequency a gemstone has and how it resonates with our own physical body. The other level of impact is our own knowledge and consciousness in action, which we implement by anchoring a specific state into a stone or piece of jewelry.

For example, when you choose a piece of Ruby jewelry and learn that Ruby is a stone that teaches you about love and self-love, you will always be unconsciously in contact with those feelings and move toward implementing those important concepts in your life. You can also create a ritual with your jewelry and anchor into it whatever principle pleases you. You could program self-confidence, peace of mind, joy, concentration, love, or whatever state would support you into the piece. (See Chapter 11 for more information on how to do that.)

Reconnecting with Mother Earth

In most Western countries, we have been brought up using all the resources we need and want without much consideration for the long-term effects on our environment. We take oil out of the ground and use it up. We mine minerals and metals and do whatever we want with them. We pollute the air and the oceans without much thought. Our world, our earthly home, provides us with so much abundance in so many ways.

Some cultures, such as Native Americans, refer to the Earth as Mother Earth, perceiving it as a living organism. When I saw the first pictures looking back at our beautiful blue planet from outer space, I felt deeply touched by the mystery of our existence.

For me, gemstones carry this mystery, abundance, and beauty of Mother Earth. They are messengers of the Divine Mother, dispensing nourishment and healing for all the needs we might have.

Gemstones are a gift to be valued and honored. Much human toil and hardship is involved in mining, cutting, and polishing stones before they end up in a shop for our admiration. If we value them as precious gifts, they can open us up to a new perception of the world. The best way to value gemstones is to enjoy them thoroughly! Play with them, meditate with them, have them set into jewelry and wear them—don't just put them away in your safe. Let them touch you and be in your life.

Having said all that, how can I not feel gratitude looking at the abundance of nature on our beautiful home planet? Sitting at the beach, listening to the waves rolling in and being pulled back out to sea, seeing the deep blue of the water meeting the clear sky at the horizon, hiking in the woods, or just sitting in a flower-filled garden are such wonderful ways to find quiet and serenity.

Being in nature is the easiest way to relax and unwind from our fast-paced lives. At those moments I feel deep gratitude for my life and all that surrounds me. I am filled with contentment and everything in my life seems just right.

Sparkling gemstones bringing colorful reflections into my life are a reminder of the immense beauty and mystery in my life and all around me. Bringing gemstones into my energy field, wearing them on my body, lifts me up and fills my heart with joy and gratitude.

6

Discovering Your
Twelve Stepping Stones
for Transformation

So far, we have learned the basics of astrology and birth charts, looked at a sample chart interpretation, and covered the various ways gemstones can benefit us and connect us to Mother Earth. In this chapter you will learn how to apply the principles of astrology in order to understand your own birth chart more deeply. Our mission in investigating your birth chart is to determine the most important themes of your life, represented by the planetary principles, in order to choose gemstones that will support you. Armed with that information, you will be able to go to a jeweler to examine the stones that you have identified as important and find stones that feel just right to you.

Stepping Stones Through the Garden of Life

A well-lived life, carried out with passion and joy, begins with a vision of where you want to go. From your vision, you develop a plan, a set of actions that can take you to your goal. I like to imagine my life's journey as a lush garden full of beautiful plants and flowers. A path laid with stepping stones winds its way through my garden to a hidden place in the center, an inner sanctuary. This is the place that I long for, a place of peace, contentment, and fulfillment. The stepping stones have been placed along the path to support and guide me as I make my way, slowly but surely, toward my inner sanctuary. I am free to use those stepping stones, or I may meander more freely as I try to find the best way to reach the life and state of being that I desire.

The life journey does not come easily to most people. It is fraught with challenges and problems to be solved. We all need help and support as we try to come to terms with the events that come our way. Our guideposts along the way may include teachers, the teachings of a specific spiritual belief system, nature, grace, and many other sources of strength and wisdom that we will find if we are vigilant. With awareness and effort, with courage and patience, we discover unexpected solutions, insights, help, and healing.

In my own life, guidance and grace have often come to me through the world of gemstones. Gemstones help me to turn my focus inward, where I have found a reservoir of strength and wisdom. This is why I call your twelve most powerful and healing stones the "stepping stones." If you will allow them, they can guide you and connect you with your rich internal resources. They are anxious to accompany you on your journey of growth and transformation.

The Ten Planets and Their Signs, Houses, and Aspects

In Chapters 3 and 4 you learned the basics of reading a birth chart. In this chapter we will look more deeply into interpreting the chart, including the meaning of the houses. You may refer back to Chapter 2 for a description of the principles associated with each planet.

On the facing page is the chart of Anne, born at 4:12 a.m. on May 21, 1957, in Berlin, Germany.

There is a correlation between the twelve star signs (Aries, Taurus, Gemini, and so on), the twelve houses (numbered 1 through 12), and the planets. The first sign, Aries, "rules" the First House, giving it its underlying qualities in addition to the sign that the house is in. Aries is also ruled by Mars, thereby lending Mars qualities to any body residing

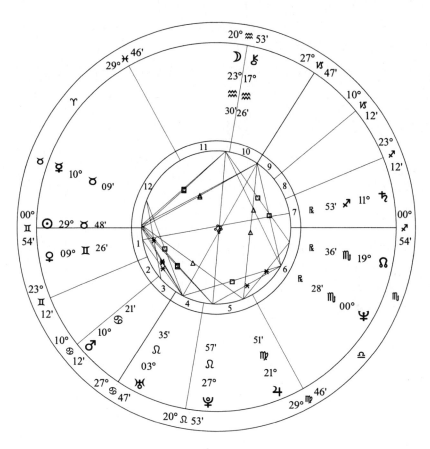

Anne
May 21, 1957 / 4:12 a.m. / Berlin, Germany

in the First House. The correlations among the star signs, houses, and planets are as follows:

SIGNS, HOUSES, AND RULING PLANETS

Sign	House	Ruling Planet
Aries	1st	Mars
Taurus	2nd	Venus
Gemini	3rd	Mercury
Cancer	4th	Moon
Leo	5th	Sun
Virgo	6th	Mercury
Libra	7th	Venus
Scorpio	8th	Pluto
Sagittarius	9th	Jupiter
Capricorn	10th	Saturn
Aquarius	11th	Uranus
Pisces	12th	Neptune

Remember that the connecting lines on your chart show particularly important aspects (relationships) among the planets, such as opposition, conjunction, and square aspects. You will want to pay special attention to the hard aspects on your chart, because they point to areas of friction.

The next section outlines the position of the planets in Anne's chart and explains how those positions influence her life and her personality. You will see that her chart reveals a number of skills and strengths that will inspire her throughout her lifetime, but also some difficulties that have indeed troubled her.

We begin our interpretation of the birth chart by noting what astrological sign and house position the Sun is in and how the Sun relates to the other planets. Do the same for each of the planets and the Moon Node on your own chart, generating a list similar to the one below. This may be difficult at first, but with practice, you will be able to combine the different planetary influences into meaningful statements.

The most important aspects to note are opposition (σ^{o}) and square (□) aspects. It is not imperative that you work with the quincunx[1] (⊼) and sextile[2] (✶) aspects, so those appear in parentheses on the list.

1. The **Sun** is in Taurus, in the Twelfth House, and has a square aspect to Pluto. As you can see on the chart above, Taurus is ruled by Venus, while Neptune rules the Twelfth House. Therefore the position of the Sun, showing its relation to the other planets, is expressed as Sun~Venus~Neptune~Pluto. This juxtaposition indicates that Anne is a very practical person with a good artistic sense and the ability to create real things from invisible dimensions. She has a deep longing to serve others, help humankind, and transform and grow into her best self. The Pluto and Neptune connections indicate Anne's constant longing and searching for the divine and deep processes of letting go and transformation throughout life.

2. The **Moon** is in Aquarius, in the Eleventh House, standing in opposition to Pluto, with a square aspect to the Sun: Moon~Uranus~Pluto~Sun. According to Anne's chart, she's a great friend to have because she values friendship (Eleventh House). She takes care of her friends and stands up for them. The Pluto opposition brings in continual self-questioning and self-critiquing. It also points to a difficult relationship with Anne's mother. This Moon position shows that she is a person who hasn't gotten as much nurturing as she may have needed.

3. **Venus** is in Taurus, in the First House, opposition Saturn: Venus~Mars~Saturn. Venus is very close to the Ascendant and therefore at the beginning of the First House. This position has a powerful impact and indicates major life themes, including creative artistic expression and placing high value on love and harmony.

....

1 "Quincunx" indicates a 150° relationship between two planets.

2 "Sextile" indicates a 60° relationship between two planets.

4. **Mercury** is in Taurus, in the Twelfth House, quincunx Saturn, sextile Mars: Mercury~Venus~Neptune (~Saturn~Mars). This shows that Anne has a very solid, practically oriented mind (Mercury) with a deep psychic connection to the invisible realms (Neptune). This seems to be a dichotomy and that is exactly the challenge of someone with this configuration: to find a way to combine a very grounded and practical way of thinking with a psychic sensitivity and connectedness to spiritual realms.

5. **Mars** is in Cancer, Third House, quincunx Saturn, sextile Mercury: Mars~Moon~Mercury (~ Saturn~Mercury). Anne's energetic expression flows very well in the area of communication, but this configuration points to a more fragile life force on a physical level.

6. **Jupiter** is in Virgo, Fifth House, quincunx Moon: Jupiter~Mercury~Sun (~Moon). This explains Anne's tendency toward self-expression aimed at what is important in the bigger picture and gives deeper meaning to her life. She has a great potential for creativity and to be acknowledged and celebrated for it.

7. **Saturn** is in Sagittarius, Seventh House, opposition Venus, quincunx Mercury, quincunx Mars: Saturn~Jupiter~Venus~Venus (~Mercury~Mars). This points to Anne's challenge in the area of relationships with hardship and heartbreaks until the inner lover is found and love is no longer perceived as a source outside the self.

8. **Uranus** is in Leo, Fourth House, sextile Sun: Uranus~Moon (~Sun). This indicates that Anne experienced changes and interruptions in childhood, such as being taken away from her family of origin. This might also be manifested in someone's life through adoption, neglect, or lack of availability of a parent for any reason.

9. **Neptune** is in Scorpio, Sixth House, quincunx Sun: Neptune~Mercury (~Sun). This configuration reveals Anne's spiritual longing and searching for God and the divine. Her chart shows that there is always something missing in her heart, even though she may find beauty in the world and success on many levels. Her mission throughout her life will be to find love and oneness.

10. **Pluto** is in Leo, Fifth House, opposition Moon, square Sun, sextile Neptune: Pluto~Sun~Moon~Sun (~Neptune). Pluto is a major influence in Anne's personality. Pluto urges us to be continually growing into our higher self. A strong Pluto influence is manifested as a life with constant deep changes and challenges to finally come to a place of nonattachment and letting go in many ways.

11. **Chiron** is in Aquarius, Eleventh House, conjunction Moon: Chiron~Uranus~Moon. Chiron shows our greatest wounds from childhood and therefore where we need to do our healing work. We see here again Anne's absent mother and her lack of nurturing and support in childhood. But her Chiron position also shows that her own healing journey may help her to become a healer and teacher for others.

12. The **Moon Node** is in Scorpio: Pluto. Anne's destiny in this incarnation is in transformation and becoming free of earthly bounds. The phoenix is the highest symbol for the deeply transformed Scorpio, who is no longer bound to the Earth, but soaring free in the sky as the young bird rises out of the ashes of transformation and death. This could be seen as the manifestation of a true human being fully realized in her potential, grounded in her knowledge and experience of oneness with all that is.

The list like the above that you generate for your own birth chart will show the most important principles at work in your life. These principles guide your life, creating potentials and challenges. The interconnections among the planets and their corresponding principles reveal in great detail your deepest desires, resources, and destiny.

Once you understand your birth chart and have generated your list of planetary positions, the hardest part of your work is done. You will be ready to go to the cross-reference list at the end of the chapter and look up the gemstones that correspond to the planetary principles you have identified as being the most powerful in your life. Remember that the hard aspects (conjunctions, squares, and oppositions) on your chat represent your areas of challenge. Be sure to include those principles when you consult the gemstone chart.

If this seems too complex and you feel you would like assistance, you can also order a **Birthstone Profile** from me. See my website, www .jewelryandgemsforselfdiscovery.com, for a sample. You may send your date, exact time, and place of birth to me at shakti@shaktijewelry.com and for $35 I will send you a complete Birthstone Profile, listing your twelve main healing and transformational stepping stones.

The Signature of the Gemstones for Your Planets

Now we will use the twelve-part list generated from Anne's birth chart above to find specific healing stones on the cross-reference list. On the list below, I have abbreviated the information from Anne's chart to include only the main planet (in bold) and the planets that stand in relation to it.

Remember that it is important to look for a stone that has at least two of the principles involved. Focus first on the most important principles, representing your main areas of challenge.

1. **Sun**~Venus~Neptune~Pluto: The most challenging principles here are Neptune and Pluto. On the list, look under Neptune and Pluto for a stone that incorporates both planets. Then look for an additional representation under the Sun and Venus.

   The chart indicates that the Herkimer Diamond is the stone that incorporates all of the principles of Neptune,

Pluto, the Sun, and Venus. The Opal Matrix, Black Opal, and Boulder Opal are also a close match. These four stones are the strongest healing stones for Anne's Sun position.

2. **Moon~Uranus~Pluto~Sun:** As above, the Herkimer Diamond and Opals incorporate the principles of the Sun and Pluto. In addition, the Crystal Clear Fire Opal corresponds to Uranus and Pluto in connection with the Moon, also a close match.

3. **Venus~Mars~Saturn:** The cross-reference list points to the Sapphire, especially the Black Star, Blue, and Green Sapphires, as well as the Diamond and the Green Diamond.

4. **Mercury~Venus~Neptune (~Saturn~Mars):** The Opals and the Tourmaline correspond to the properties of these planets.

5. **Mars~Moon~Mercury (~Saturn~Mercury):** Here we find the Aquamarine, the Demantoid, and the Black Sapphire. I wouldn't choose the Opals here because there is no involvement of Pluto, Uranus, or Neptune.

   (The Opals with their color variations include all of the planetary principles, depending on their colors, but they are most helpful for the outer planets and their combinations with the inner planets.)

6. **Jupiter~Mercury~Sun (~Moon):** The Golden Beryl (Heliodor), Yellow Sapphire, Tsavorite Garnet, and Orange-Pink Sapphire are good matches for these principles.

7. **Saturn~Jupiter~Venus~Venus (~Mercury~Mars):** The Black Star Sapphire, Blue Sapphire, and Green Diamond incorporate the properties of these planets.

8. **Uranus~Moon (~Sun):** Aquamarine, all of the Opals, Moonstone, Herkimer Diamond, and Labradorite are good matches. I would strongly recommend using the Opals and the Herkimer Diamond first because they are the strongest allies for the process of transformation.

9. **Neptune**~Mercury (~Sun): We have quite a few choices here: all of the Opals, Bixbite, Rainbow Moonstone, Pearls, Tanzanite, Tourmaline, and Violet Sapphire. Again, the Opals would be the first choice that I would recommend.

10. **Pluto**~Sun~Moon~Sun (~Neptune): I strongly recommend Opals and Herkimer Diamonds for any Pluto connection.

11. **Chiron**~Uranus~Moon: One stone stands out: the Blue Moonstone.

12. **Moon Node**~Pluto: Here again, the Opal in all its beauty and diversity is the first choice.

Make a list of all the stones you have identified so far as incorporating the most important principles that you want to work with at present in your life, according to your current challenges. If a planet is repeated several times in your chart, this points toward issues that you need to pay particular attention to. Stones that correspond to that planet should be at the top of your list. Now you're ready for a visit to a jeweler or a gemstone shop to begin selecting or designing your healing jewelry!

Relating Anne's Birth Chart to Her Jewelry

You can see above that Opals appear again and again in the astrological configurations on Anne's chart. And, indeed, throughout her life she has loved and collected many pieces with Australian and Mexican Opals. She particularly loved a ring with an Australian Boulder Opal and a Diamond accent stone.

Anne and I created the *Mother Earth & Father Sky* ring on page A10 mainly for her Sun position with her challenging Pluto and Neptune aspects. Because of its almost electric turquoise blue, this specific Opal has also very strong Uranus qualities; it will also help pacify her Moon in Aquarius in the Eleventh House in conjunction with the Chiron, opposition Pluto. In this way we have elegantly touched on two major actors in her chart—Sun, the masculine, and Moon, the feminine principle.

On the surface of the Opal, you can see the mother matrix and how it is interwoven with the intense fire and sparkle of the opalescent reflection. I called this ring *Mother Earth & Father Sky* to convey how we are children of both, born out of Heaven and Earth and influenced by both.

With Opal's never-ending potential for transformation and healing, this stone especially touches the heart and the throat chakra with the green and blue color. We can see the depth of the ocean and our spirit and soul reflected in the limitless sky.

The asymmetrical setting of the Diamond appealed to Anne's Uranian sense of balance. As you can tell, she is a gold person[3] and loves the soft, harmonizing forms and stones, which help her to counterbalance the friction in her chart. But she needs an unusual element in her designs to satisfy the position of her Moon in Uranus—Uranus, a trendsetter, always seeks the extraordinary. Still, the main intent here is for balance and harmony.

Anne got this ring in a time of a strong Mars/Saturn transit. So we used gold for the head and iron (Mars) for the blackened (Saturn) ring shank as an added bonus, which also satisfied her preference for the unusual (Uranus).

The ring on page A8, which I call *Expanding Heart*, is one of Anne's favorites. It has two kinds of Mexican Fire Opal accented by two Diamonds. The Diamond accent stones bring in the whole rainbow of colors and help to integrate and spread the transformational impact of the Fire Opals throughout the body. These Opals show a lot of green, gold, orange, and red, which is an unusual and wonderful combination for the heart and belly. This ring is meant to soothe the heart and transform blockages in the energetic and chakra system.

People who are attracted to the passionate Mexican Fire Opals often have outer-planet themes in their chart. You can see how often Opals and the theme of transformation are appearing for Anne.

....

3 See Chapter 9 to find out whether you are a gold or a silver person.

If there is an attraction to the Fire Opal, there is always a need to strengthen the Mars or fire element in general. Anne's Mars is in Cancer (water) and she has Saturn with his blocking energies in a fire sign, in Sagittarius. That points toward a more fragile life force in general.

In the end, Anne decided on the Fire Opals for her Mars instead of a design with Aquamarine, Demantoid, or the Black Sapphire, which would also have been good choices.

In designing an open ring shank we used an unusual form of two opposing, different but similar stones. It could be said that the golden Fire Opal stimulates the heart and its longing to flower into its highest form of love and the experience of oneness, while the dark, redder Fire Opal helps to unblock the first three chakras, guiding the Kundalini up to the heart.

The Herkimer Diamond in the pendant on page A11, which I call *Power of the Soul*, appears several times in Anne's Sun, Moon, Uranus, and Pluto positions. Anne loved this pendant made by my husband Will. Worn over the heart, it is designed to bridge and pacify polarities, strengthen the aura, and center the wearer in the heart.

This is a beautiful example of jewelry made with a Herkimer Diamond, a natural crystal that is not used frequently by jewelers. They are treasures and not easy to come by, but it is possible to find them. The Herkimer Diamond is a beautiful specimen, as it has been created by nature. It has not been cut or polished in any way. Usually, the Herkimers are much smaller in size than this exceptional piece. Here we had the opportunity to add additional cut and polished gemstones to the design to incorporate different healing qualities into one piece.

I always like the look of natural crystals in combination with polished stones. There is something powerful about the refinement of polished gems done by the human hand in contrast to the natural crystal birthed by nature.

This pendant also features a Tanzanite (Neptune), Rubellite (Mercury), and a little Diamond (Sun), a combination that works very well for Anne. The Tanzanite helps to connect her to spiritual guidance, higher truth, and consciousness. The Rubellite is also a very meaningful stone for her because it awakens the heart to self-love and is very sooth-ing. Anne can use some soothing energy with so many Pluto, Neptune, and Uranus challenges in her life! Her tendency is to be too critical of herself. Diamond always serves very well to pull all the energies together and integrate all the different frequencies because it represents the whole array of the rainbow.

You can see from the above that once you have analyzed your chart many possibilities emerge for corresponding jewelry to your planetary configurations. You can be creative in playing with all of the informa-tion you have at your fingertips now.

This might all sound complicated, but, in fact, it isn't. If you walk through the process step by step with your own horoscope in hand, everything will start to make sense. And you also have the choice of having me do the work or comparing your own results with my Birth-stone Profile.

It can be a lot of fun to play with your chart this way while achiev-ing a deeper understanding of your potential and destiny. Enjoy your journey of revelation as you choose the right stepping stones for your own garden path.

Gemstones for Your Destiny
Represented by the North Moon Node

One of the most healing stones out of the twelve main gemstones is the one we pick for the position of our North Node. This stone rep-resents our destiny in a spiritual sense. It represents our karmic goal and intent on a soul level. It can help us remember that we are eternal spiritual beings having a human experience and remind us of what we want to learn and grow to be in this lifetime. Your North Node gem-stone corresponds to where the North Node is found in your chart:

NORTH NODE (☊) GEMSTONES

Position of North Node in Chart	Gemstone
Aries	Ruby
Taurus	Demantoid or Green Diamond
Gemini	Tourmaline
Cancer	Pearl or Moonstone
Leo	Diamond
Virgo	Yellow Sapphire
Libra	Emerald
Scorpio	Opal
Sagittarius	Tanzanite
Capricorn	Black Star Sapphire
Aquarius	Aquamarine
Pisces	Amethyst

Gemstones for Your Chiron Position

Chiron is not one of the official ancient ten planets mainly used in Western astrology, but it has special meaning for astrologers. Chiron was discovered in 1977 orbiting between Saturn and Uranus. Due to its small size it is called a "planetoid"; it has a tail and is considered to be both an asteroid and a comet.

Chiron is named for the centaur—half horse and half human—of Greek legend. Chiron was a healer and a teacher of the healing arts. He was accidentally wounded with an arrow and his wound, which was incurable, caused him such great pain that he wished to die. Being immortal, he could not die. He proposed to Zeus, king of the gods, that he should trade his immortality for the release of Prometheus, at that time chained to a boulder on Mount Caucasus as punishment for having stolen fire from the gods and given it to humankind. Zeus accepted this trade and Chiron became mortal and died, as was his wish. He was then transformed by Zeus into the constellation Centaurus.

Thus we think of Chiron as the wounded healer. Chiron represents our greatest wounds, the parts of ourselves and our lives that are in need of healing, and therefore, to my mind, Chiron has great importance in astrology. By drawing our attention to our wounds, Chiron can serve as a guide, teacher, and healer, inviting us to find the gift of healing through understanding and integration of higher truth into our life.

Through our own suffering and journey of self-healing, we learn a great deal about ourselves and in the end we often become compassionate healers and competent teachers in our own areas of challenge. I have seen many charts of people in the physical and psychological healing professions with a prominent Chiron position.

To speak personally, I myself have a very close conjunction between my Moon (nurturing qualities) and my Chiron (healing from wounds). My Moon is already very challenged by a square between Pluto and my ascendant. My birth mother suffered from mental illness. I spent the first four months of my life in a hospital with her, and then was raised by my aunt and uncle, who I knew as loving parents. When I was twelve years old, my birth mother kidnapped me and forced me to go live with her. The sudden separation from the loving people who had raised me was very traumatic. This deep wound in the area of childhood attachment and nurturing is indicated by the conjunction of the Moon and Chiron in my chart.

All my life, from an early age, I have been interested in psychology, religion, and other areas related to human nature. I was pushed early on into my own process of healing and embarked on a journey through many teachings and therapeutic processes. My main motivation was to get better, to find something that would heal me and eliminate my suffering. Along the way I learned much about alternative ways of healing. Finally I created my own way of bringing healing to others through the beauty and healing properties of gemstones in my jewelry and through my astrological readings. In this sense my wound has become my calling. In this way, Chiron can motivate us to do great good while healing our own wounds.

The following chart shows the useful gemstones for a Chiron position in each star sign.

CHIRON (⚷) GEMSTONES

Sign	Gemstone
Aries	Amethyst
Taurus	Emerald
Gemini	Crystal Quartz
Cancer	Herkimer Diamond
Leo	Amber
Virgo	Beryl
Libra	Tourmaline
Scorpio	Opal
Sagittarius	Jade
Capricorn	Black Pearl
Aquarius	Moonstone
Pisces	Pearl

Cross–Reference Guide to Gemstones, Signs, and Planetary Principles

The following chart shows how star signs, planets, and gemstones relate to each other. The star signs are listed across the top of the chart. Below the star signs, the symbols show which planets are associated with each stone in the star signs.

The chart can be used in two ways. If you know what your main spiritual needs are, you can find a stone that is associated with those planetary principles. Or, if you find a stone that particularly appeals to you, you can look it up on the chart to discover its astrological qualities and determine whether that stone would support your current needs.

Gemstones, Star Signs, & Their Planetary Influences

Gemstones	Aries ♈	Taurus ♉	Gemini ♊	Cancer ♋	Leo ♌	Virgo ♍	Libra ♎	Scorpio ♏	Sagittarius ♐	Capricorn ♑	Aquarius ♒	Pisces ♓	Chiron ⚷
Alexandrite	♂	♀	☿			☿	♀		♃				
Amber			☿		☉	☿			♃				⚷
Amethyst	♂								♃			♆	⚷
Apatite			☿		☉	☿			♃				
Apophyllite	♂	♀		☽			♀		♃			♆	⚷
Aquamarine			☿	☽		☿					♅		
Azurite		♀	☿			☿	♀		♃	♄		♆	⚷
Beryl	♂	♀	☿		☉	☿	♀		♃			♆	⚷
Bixbite	♂	♀	☿		☉	☿	♀		♃			♆	⚷
Goshenite			☿		☉	☿	♀				♅		
Heliodor		♀	☿		☉	☿	♀		♃				⚷
Morganite		♀		☽			♀					♆	⚷
Bloodstone	♂	♀					♀						
Carnelian	♂			☽	☉								⚷
Chrysoberyl		♀		☽	☉		♀		♃			♆	⚷
Chrysocolla		♀	☿			☿	♀				♅		

Gemstones, Star Signs, & Their Planetary Influences continued

Gemstones	Aries ♈	Taurus ♉	Gemini ♊	Cancer ♋	Leo ♌	Virgo ♍	Libra ♎	Scorpio ♏	Sagittarius ♐	Capricorn ♑	Aquarius ♒	Pisces ♓	Chiron ⚷
Chrysoprase		♀		☽			♀		♃				⚷
Citrine			☿		☉	☿							
Diamond	♂	♀	☿		☉	☿	♀			♄	♅		
Green	♂	♀			☉		♀		♃	♄			
Yellow		♀	☿		☉	☿	♀		♃	♄			
Diopside									♃	♄			
Dioptase		♀		☽			♀		♃				
Emerald		♀	☿	☽		☿	♀		♃				⚷
Garnet	♂	♀	☿	☽			♀		♃	♄			
Almandine	♂	♀	☿			☿	♀		♃			♆	
Demantoid	♂	♀		☽			♀		♃				
Golden	♂	♀			☉		♀		♃				
Grossular	♂	♀					♀		♃				
Pyrope	♂	♀					♀			♄			
Spessartite	♂	♀					♀			♄			
Tsavorite		♀	☿		☉	☿	♀		♃				

	♂	♀	☿	☽	☉	☿	♀	♆	♃	♄	♅	♃	☋
Herkimer Diamond	♂	♀	☿		☉	☿				♄	♅		
Jade		♀		☽			♀		♃			♃	
Labradorite			☿	☽		☿			♃	♄	♅	♃	
Lapis Lazuli			☿			☿			♃	♄		♃	
Moonstone		♀	☿	☽		☿	♀				♅	♃	☋
Opal	♂	♀	☿	☽			♀	♆		♄	♅	♃	
Black	♂						♀	♆		♄	♅	♃	
Boulder		♀	☿			☿	♀	♆		♄	♅	♃	
Matrix		♀	☿			☿		♆		♄	♅	♃	
Crystal Clear Fire				☽				♆			♅	♃	
Fire	♂	♀					♀	♆				♃	
Lightning Ridge			☿			☿		♆		♄	♅	♃	
White				☽				♆			♅	♃	
Pearl				☽						♄		♃	☋
Black				☽						♄		♃	☋
Peridot		♀			☉		♀		♃				
Quartz			☿		☉	☿				♄			☋

Gemstones, Star Signs, & Their Planetary Influences continued

Gemstones	*Aries* ♈	*Taurus* ♉	*Gemini* ♊	*Cancer* ♋	*Leo* ♌	*Virgo* ♍	*Libra* ♎	*Scorpio* ♏	*Sagittarius* ♐	*Capricorn* ♑	*Aquarius* ♒	*Pisces* ♓	Chiron ⚷
Ruby	♂	♀			☉		♀					♆	
Star	♂	♀			☉		♀					♆	
Sapphire	♂	♀	☿			☿	♀		♃	♄			
Black Star	♂	♀					♀	♇		♄			
Blue	♂	♀	☿			☿	♀		♃	♄	♅		
Green	♂	♀					♀		♃	♄			
Orange-Pink		♀	☿		☉	☿	♀		♃				
Pink		♀					♀		♃			♆	
Violet		♀	☿			☿	♀		♃			♆	
Yellow		♀	☿		☉	☿	♀		♃				
Spinel	♂	♀			☉		♀					♆	
Tanzanite			☿			☿			♃	♄		♆	
Tourmaline	♂	♀	☿			☿	♀		♃			♆	
Green		♀					♀		♃				
Indigolite/Paraiba		♀	☿			☿	♀		♃			♆	
Rubellite	♂	♀	☿			☿	♀					♆	
Watermelon	♂	♀	☿			☿	♀						
Zircon			☿			☿					♅		

7

Guide to Gemstones and Crystals

Physical and Metaphysical Properties

With the help of the previous chapters, you have identified the gemstones that are your main guiding or stepping stones through your beautiful garden of life. You should have a list of at least twelve or more stones. In this chapter, you will enjoy the next step: reading about your selected stones, discovering how you resonate with the descriptions, and deciding which stones would best serve your needs at this time.

Many people going through this process find old acquaintances or loves on their list of gemstones. You may have loved Amethysts all your life; this chapter may well help you understand why your heart has always been drawn to that gemstone.

The stones are listed below in alphabetical order, followed by their associated planets to help you discover the astrological characteristics of each stone. A color photo of some stones is also included on pages A1–A12. Keep in mind that gems can vary greatly in color and form. Some stones are featured in photos of finished jewelry pieces, which is noted in the stone's profile in this chapter. This is just a sampling of the most common gemstones—you may find other stones that speak to your soul.

Alexandrite

MARS ♂, VENUS ♀, MERCURY ☿, JUPITER ♃

Alexandrite is one of the most astonishing gems because it changes its color from green in daylight to red in artificial light. Alexandrite is a variety of Chrysoberyl and is very rare and expensive. Today it is mined mainly in Sri Lanka and Rhodesia.

This is a stone for the queen or king in us because of its great value, both monetary and metaphysical.

As it changes from green to red, Alexandrite shows us that our so-called objective perception of the world of objects may change drastically by shining a different light on it, encouraging us to view experiences from other points of view. This gemstone strengthens the heart by opening our awareness of different perspectives. It reminds us that it is never the experience itself that is good or bad; what is important is our perception, evaluation, and judgment of events.

Alexandrite stays by our side as a faithful friend, helping us through transitions in our relationships with friends and loved ones. It nourishes the heart during the process of grieving and letting go of a beloved one, whether our loss is due to death or other forms of separation.

Amber

MERCURY ☿, SUN ☉, JUPITER ♃, CHIRON ⚷

Amber is special because it is the only gemstone that comes to us from the plant world. Amber is the fossilized, hardened resin of pine trees that formed about fifty million years ago. It has an amorphous (non crystalline) structure. It is found in various places, with the largest reserve in Samland, a region of Russia on the Baltic Sea near the border of Poland. Usually the color of amber is in the yellow-orange to brown range, but there are also varieties in white, black, blue, and greenish colors. We refer here to the yellow-orange variety because it is the most common.

Amber has the ability to create static electricity when it is rubbed with a cloth. This ability makes it a healer for harmonizing the electrical fields in and around our physical body. Amber balances our hormonal, nervous, and digestive systems.

Amber belongs to the third chakra, the solar plexus area. Here it softens and releases tensions and the physical manifestations of fears, which may include a tight, sour, or upset stomach.

By connecting us with the powerful life-force energy of the Sun, Amber brings us vibrant, joyful aliveness. Universally, people enjoy spending time in the Sun and bathing the body in its life-giving energy. This is one of the oldest naturally occurring meditations, the Sun meditation, which induces in us a deep state of inward-turned relaxation. Amber also relieves depression by connecting us with our own inner Sun center, our internal spark of light and joy. It enhances creativity, personal strength, self-expression, and power.

Amber is also a wonderful stone for babies, making them happy and joyful. An old German home remedy is to give a baby a large piece to bite on to relieve the pain of teething!

Amethyst
MARS ♂, JUPITER ♃, NEPTUNE ♆, CHIRON ⚷

Amethyst is a very common six-sided, pale- to dark-violet crystal of the Quartz family. It originates most commonly in Brazil, Uruguay, and Madagascar. The quality and depth of color of the stone vary widely. The most desirable and clearest material will be cut as facetted (cut along flat faces) or cabochon (dome shaped, polished) stones.

Amethyst is an excellent stone to use to introduce yourself to the subtle energies of crystals. It comes in huge clusters large enough to contain your hand. In fact at gem shows I have seen bathtub-shaped pieces that were large enough to lie in! When you put your hand into one of these clusters, you feel a pulsating sensation similar to an ultrasound device. I had a huge sample of Amethyst in my studio in Germany that I used to provide my clients with an immediate experience of crystal energy.

Large Amethyst clusters function as a sort of "spiritual vacuum cleaner," cleansing rooms with a lot of traffic. They are also perfect for cleaning other stones or jewelry, which can be done by simply laying the objects in the Amethyst cluster.

In olden times, Amethyst was known as an amulet against black magic and homesickness, and as a bringer of good fortune. I see Amethyst as Merlin, the old sorcerer who looks harmless enough but in fact wields great power. In the myth, he was the spiritual teacher and magician of King Arthur.

Amethyst can become our individual teacher as well. This gem's greatest gift is its ability to open us up to higher realms of reality, higher states of consciousness. It enhances meditation, connecting us with our higher self and the supreme reality.

The meaning of the Greek name for Amethyst is "not drunken," and it is considered to aid sobriety. When we access higher planes of consciousness, where we feel ourselves held, comforted, and nourished, our longing for the anesthetizing effects of substances such as alcohol and drugs slowly dissipates as we become open to a more enjoyable and beautiful experience.

When there is a strong influence of Neptune in our chart, there is an ever present yearning for a higher realm of consciousness, a longing for God, a search for something more than our daily reality. People who fall under this astrological configuration are often tempted to take a shortcut to that plane by using chemical substances to escape reality. But their efforts fail in the long run because they are disappointed by the false world of chemical highs.

By uplifting our consciousness, Amethyst becomes the messenger who reminds us of our eternal connection with God. It is the bringer of bliss and understanding, of expansion to our being. It helps to clear the mind and to transform our limiting beliefs about who we are. It is our guardian and ally who accompanies us on our visionary quest to find greater truth and meaning in life.

See the photo of *Divine Love* on page A7 for an example of Amethyst jewelry.

Apatite
MERCURY ☿, SUN ☉, JUPITER ♃

Apatite is a beautiful stone occurring in a great variety of colors, including white, pink, yellow, green, blue, and violet. The more common colors are the yellow-greenish hues. The crystals are hexagonal and short; it may also be found in the form of a cat's eye. Its origins include Burma, Brazil, and Sri Lanka. It is not a good stone to set into rings because it is brittle and has a hardness of 5 on the Mohs' scale, which is relatively soft, making it not rugged enough for a ring.

Apatite has a pleasing shine and a very soft, warm, and soothing radiance.

Its soft light sets up a healing, nourishing energy flow between the solar plexus and the heart chakra. In strengthening our own creative expression in alignment with the heart, it helps us to create and express ourselves from our deepest truth. In this sense, this is a stone for artists and people who want to activate the energy of the solar plexus chakra (the "power" chakra) to achieve their innermost dreams.

The great variety of colors of Apatite reminds us of the importance of our inner as well as outer abundance.

Apophyllite
VENUS ♀, MOON ☽, JUPITER ♃, NEPTUNE ♆, CHIRON ⚷

Apophyllite is a very rare, light-green, four-sided, diamond-faced crystal found in only one place on the Earth: Poona, India. The Poona mine was closed after some years of operation due to citizens' objections to the dynamiting in the middle of their city; thus this is a very rare stone and good pieces are hard to find nowadays.

I love this stone because of its unique generous qualities for the heart. In its natural crystallized form it can be set into beautiful pendants and worn right over the heart. This is a stone for the heart chakra and connects us to love in its highest form.

This energy is focused in our heart and connects us with the quality of compassion as a result of realizing who we really are: eternal spiritual beings of love, experiencing ourselves as humans on this earthly plane.

The light color of Apophyllite is soft and gentle, almost like a fragrance, and its energy is very subtle, soothing, and expanding. The heart's longing is to experience communion and oneness with God, with life in all its facets. It is the longing of the soul to melt the shell around the heart and heal its wounds, and compassion is the natural outcome of this process.

The planet Chiron represents the wounded healer. Chiron shows us our deepest hurt on the astrological chart. He shows us where we need to heal ourselves and where we can become a healer for others as a result of our own experience. Chiron and Neptune are hand in hand, joining their energies together to help us experience the highest truth of love and compassion: this is what we call "Higher Consciousness," or "Christ Consciousness."

Apophyllite also may bring up emotions that are not in line with the Christ Consciousness. It may work as an accelerator of spiritual growth by helping us to cleanse ourselves of grief, anger, jealousy, and fear—all the so-called negative emotions—by realigning ourselves with the truth that we are divine consciousness.

This crystal is one of the most powerful healers for the heart and thus it is a stone for healers. It is very beneficial to wear this beautiful, unique gem over the heart. For meditation, you may put it on your third eye or on your heart chakra. It goes very well together with the Ruby or Spinel, which add other aspects of the heart.

Aquamarine

MARS ♂, MERCURY ☿, MOON ☽, URANUS ♅

The Aquamarine, along with the Emerald, belongs to the Beryl family. It is found around the world, with the most important sources in Brazil and Madagascar. It crystallizes in a long six-sided prism. Its name derives from the Latin for "water of the ocean" because of its color, which may be light blue, medium blue, or blue-green. The most expensive and desirable color is the darkest blue.

Uranus infuses Aquamarine with some unusual qualities and a vision beyond our usually limited mind-set, making Aquamarine the rebel among the gems. This is the gemstone of visionaries fighting for a better life, supporting goodness and necessary changes. It urges us to seek freedom and independence and to express our uniqueness. Aquamarine is the stone of innovators, ahead of their time in many ways. It encourages us to always question our limiting beliefs with an open mind and to be willing to grow beyond them. It can help us to find our own vision and purpose in life and the courage to live them.

This unique gem connects us with the unlimited aspect of being that is found in the ocean, symbolizing the vastness of existence, the unlimited space and horizon that we experience standing on a beach or a boat.

Aquamarine also has a female aspect, represented by the Moon. The Moon symbolizes our unconscious mind, our emotions, and our past memories. It reflects our emotional needs and wants, our ability to give and receive. Through its female aspect, Aquamarine supports and nourishes us, as if with mother's milk. Feeling full and nurtured, we are able to share from the abundance of our own heart.

Aquamarine also sharpens our mind and our powers of discernment and helps us tap into the collective unconscious mind with all its creative resources. In so doing, it helps us develop our intuitive creativity and objective knowledge.

Aquamarine opens and balances the throat chakra, which helps us to express our personal truth, including our true feelings. The throat chakra is an area where we all have many blocks; thus we often feel limited in our self-expression.

Iron gives Aquamarine its color and energizing element. It is said to help remedy iron deficiency. With its high energy level, Aquamarine restores equilibrium in over energized people who are impatient, always rushing about, overstressed, and tense. Those individuals may be at high risk of accidents!

Aquamarine also represents Mother Mary. When we strip away two thousand years of male Christian tradition, we discover that Mary was not only the mother of Christ but a strong and highly evolved being in her own right and thus a role model for us today. Her strength also relates to the tradition of the Black Madonna that is found all over the world. The Black Madonna stands for the destructive and creative female principle of the universe, called *Shakti* in the East Indian tradition.

Thus versatile Aquamarine represents the qualities of freedom, growth, moving beyond limitations, a sharp mind, creativity, self-expression, and balance. Drawing on these qualities, Aquamarine helps women to grow into a new dimension of their womanhood and helps men to balance their own inner woman. A man who integrates these aspects of Aquamarine is able to enter into a balanced and equal relationship with a strong woman without fear of losing himself or his position.

Sky & Ocean on page A11 is a nice example of Aquamarine.

Azurite

VENUS ♀, MERCURY ☿, JUPITER ♃, SATURN ♄

As its name expresses, Azurite is a very deep blue stone with short crystals. The color belongs to the third eye chakra. Azurite can be used in its crystal form as a pendant or on the third eye for meditation.

Azurite stimulates our mind to connect to deeper truth and intuition and broadens and sharpens our perception of the world. By bringing our mind's focus to the depths of our unconscious resources, we can achieve deep insights. We learn to focus our attention on a single point without becoming distracted by dozens of conflicting thoughts.

Azurite helps us to manifest our highest thoughts into the world. It brings peace to the mind as we come to see beauty within ourselves and around us. Writers may use it to increase their work focus. Students may use its forces to concentrate on learning tasks and to stay calm and focused during examinations.

Beryl

MARS ♂, VENUS ♀, MERCURY ☿, SUN ☉,
JUPITER ♃, NEPTUNE ♆, CHIRON ⚷

Beryl is an amazing gemstone that occurs in a wide variety of colors, each variety having its own name. In addition to the well-known Emerald and Aquamarine, Beryl manifests its beauty in gold, yellow-green, yellow, pink, and a colorless variety. These stones come from many different places, including Brazil, the Malagasy Republic, Namibia, Sri Lanka, and Rhodesia. Beryl crystallizes in long hexagonal prisms. All the varieties, especially the Emerald, are very brittle and break easily if struck.

Bixbite

MARS ♂, VENUS ♀, SUN ☉, JUPITER ♃, NEPTUNE ♆, CHIRON ⚷

Bixbite is the strawberry-red Beryl. Its orange undertone conveys a fiery yet still soft disposition. It belongs to the sacral chakra and the heart chakra. It creates a connection between our sexual fire, our sensuality, and the softness of the heart. It teaches us to allow our gentleness to arise, to experience sexuality as an act of communion, melting together, riding the wave toward higher and higher states of love and consciousness expressed and felt in our physical body. We have permission to be as sensual and playful and sexual as we would like to be. Bixbite helps us to feel the life-force energy in each cell of our body, vibrating with joy and bliss. Inviting us to release tensions in the sexual organs and the intestines, it aids our digestion and helps us to integrate higher energies into the physical realm.

Bixbite is a beautiful companion and teacher for those who want to enhance and integrate more of their sexual and heart's desires. Tantra is known to use sexual desire as a path to move toward higher bliss and consciousness rather than struggling to confine our sexuality—a path of moving with the wave of bliss instead of against it. Bixbite is thus a tantric agent.

Goshenite
MERCURY ☿, SUN ☉, URANUS ♅

Goshenite is a colorless Beryl that refracts light into a magnificent rainbow of colors. It opens the crown chakra and connects us directly to the source of all light: eternal, infinite consciousness.

In antiquity, eyeglasses were made from Goshenite. Today we use it to enhance our inner sight in various ways. It prepares us for new dimensions to look at the world, helping us to find the light within and outside ourselves, because consciousness is all that is. Aided by Goshenite we may find a new direction in our spiritual search, such as joining a spiritual tradition, meeting a new teacher, or learning a new way of meditation. Our spiritual quest takes a new turn as Goshenite reveals more about our divine destiny.

Heliodor, or Golden Beryl
VENUS ♀, MERCURY ☿, SUN ☉, JUPITER ♃, CHIRON ⚷

Golden Beryl, also called Heliodor, varies between lemon yellow, golden yellow, and gold. All look very similar and bear similar gifts. In fact the name of the stone is derived from the Greek *helios,* "sun," and *doron,* "gift."

By connecting the solar plexus chakra and the heart chakra, Heliodor transmits the cheerful, strengthening energy of the Sun into our mind-body system. It allows us to tap deeply into our creativity and use it in a meaningful way.

The Sun is the source of all life and consciousness in our solar system. The most natural way of meditating is what I call Sun meditation, meaning simply lying in the sunlight and relaxing. We all long for Sun meditation, especially after a long winter.

In olden times, exposure to sunlight was a natural remedy for many diseases, which makes sense, because the Sun augments the general life-force energy, catalyzing the inner healing process. Spending time in sunlight is a very natural way to fill yourself with an abundance of life-force energy, to feel vibrant, joyful aliveness.

By tuning into and connecting with the energy of these stones, you may experience yourself as a being made of light and pure consciousness. In this way, the Golden Beryl reminds us of our true nature, of who we really are. It opens our mind to different realities and perspectives on life—for example, to perceive the good in a situation instead of the bad. It helps us to orient our mind toward solutions rather than problems. When bad things inevitably occur in our lives, it helps us to extract positive meaning and lessons from those events. We are then able to move from a negative position of lack and distress to an action position filled with creative solutions to meet our challenges.

Morganite

MOON ☽, VENUS ♀, NEPTUNE ♆, CHIRON ⚷

Morganite is the pink to violet variety of the Beryl family. This is the Divine Mother, a delight for our heart because it magnifies our ability to feel loved.

In my experience, one of the root stressors basic to our human condition is that we don't allow ourselves to be loved because of deep feelings of unworthiness, pain, and despair. We think, "If God loved me, he would not allow me to experience all this suffering, pain, and disaster. And if God doesn't love me, how could anyone else love me?" Morganite brings us the message that we long to hear: that indeed God does love us. This message of God's love becomes a deep inner spark of knowledge that sustains us in our search for a deeper, richer, more meaningful life—the longing for happiness and joy that is our heritage and our way home to our deepest selves.

Morganite is the queen among the heart stones. Its beautiful, noble appearance raises up our spirit so we may start feeling love by sharing our love. We come to understand a simple truth: that whenever we express love by caring for the plants in our garden, our children, our pets, our friends, our neighbors, and our fellow humans, we are sharing love. Morganite reminds us that we are never truly alone, for we all have the capacity to give love and care.

Bloodstone, or Heliotrope

MARS ♂, VENUS ♀

Bloodstone is a green Chalcedony (an opaque Quartz with a waxlike luster) and, as its name suggests, it has red spots that resemble blood. In the Middle Ages, it was said to be spotted with the blood of Christ and was believed to have magical powers, including the ability to stop bleeding. Women wore it during childbirth to strengthen themselves and limit the loss of blood.

Bloodstone helps us to ground ourselves on the Earth, connecting us with the spirit of nature in the world of the mineral and plant kingdoms. It opens us up to the beauty in nature and helps us to feel our roots and recharge and rejuvenate our bodies.

Carnelian

MARS ♂, MOON ☽, SUN ☉, NEPTUNE ♆, CHIRON ⚷

Carnelian, another member of the Chalcedony Quartz group, is red to red-brown. The best stones come from India, where the color is enhanced by exposing the stones to sunlight.

This stone carries great grounding and empowering energy. In the native Indian tradition, it is the stone of strength and power of the Earth. It vibrates at the same rate as the healthy body. By activating the first and second chakras, it grounds us and enhances our physical well-being through energizing, revitalizing, and balancing us. It links us to the power of the tribe, drumming and dancing around the fire, falling into a trance, finding our deep connection with Mother Earth. It is both mother and father, simultaneously nourishing, healing, and empowering us.

Carnelian is one of the rare stones that provide both great energy (Sun and Mars) and maternal soothing (Moon). I recommend that it be used in times of fatigue, recovery from illness, uncertainty, depression, or whenever you feel a need for more energy, especially to help you realize your dreams and visions on the earthly plane.

Mountain Dream on page A10 is a Carnelian piece.

Chrysoberyl

VENUS ♀, MOON ☽, SUN ☉, JUPITER ♃, NEPTUNE ♆, CHIRON ⚷

Chrysoberyl (from the Greek *chrysos*, "gold") has been appreciated since very early times. It is a very light golden, green-yellow, or sometimes brown stone; I refer here to the green-yellow variety. It grows in long prismatic, orthorhombic (having three perpendicular axes of different lengths) crystals. Deposits are found in a variety of places, including Brazil, Sri Lanka, and northern Myanmar. The variety of Alexandrite is discussed elsewhere in this chapter. Chrysoberyl Cat's Eye is an opaque stone with a soft glow reflecting light off the cabochon cut, reminiscent of an eye. It's softer and more feminine than the clear variety.

Chrysoberyl is a light-filled gem that brings us the joy of life. In its presence we experience ourselves as playful and radiant. It brings us the gift of love for life, a connection with all that is, as we feel the subtle current of the life force pulsing through our system. It also helps to release tensions and fears manifested in the solar plexus area.

Chrysoberyl bridges our consciousness with the solar consciousness, the Sun as the center of life and consciousness in this universe. Thus it opens us to dimensions far beyond our limited view of the world and our perception of ourselves here on the Earth.

Open Heart on page A10 features Chrysoberyl.

Chrysocolla

VENUS ♀, MERCURY ☿, URANUS ♅

Chrysocolla has an amorphous (noncrystalline) structure and is a fairly soft stone with a Mohs' hardness of 2–4. Its color is a mixture of blue and green. If it is intergrown with Turquoise and Malachite, it is called Eilat stone.

Because of its opaqueness, Chrysocolla channels the high energies of Uranus and makes it available to us on the Earth. By connecting the heart with the throat chakra, it helps bring to expression our deepest feelings, making this a wonderful stone for writers and artists.

Chrysocolla reminds us that we are unlimited divine beings living a human experience. It helps us to create a beautiful environment around ourselves by allowing us to feel the spirit in minerals, plants and herbs, and the animal kingdom.

Chrysoprase
VENUS ♀, MOON ☽, JUPITER ♃

Chrysoprase is another member of the Quartz family. It is hexagonal, microcrystalline, and apple-green in color. It is the most valuable stone in the Chalcedony group. Recently the best quality stones have been coming from Queensland in Australia. Because it is opaque, it is used as cabochons or ornamental objects.

Chrysoprase is one of the most soothing, nourishing, and healing stones for our heart and our emotional body. It has the mothering quality of the Moon and the balancing and loving aspects of Venus, and through Jupiter it brings the expansion of the heart and the finding of deeper meaning in painful processes. It helps to bring these qualities into the physical body and balances them there.

Chrysoprase has a very fresh and joyful energy—I almost taste mint when I meditate with this stone!

Chrysoprase balances very nicely with the Sun and Mars stones, like Diamond or Ruby, which would also bring in the brilliant light aspect when set together in jewelry.

Citrine
MERCURY ☿, SUN ☉

Citrine is a light-yellow to gold-brown Quartz. It crystallizes in hexagonal prisms with pyramids on the top of each crystal. Most Citrines found in shops are heat-treated Amethysts or Smoky Quartzes. The treated stones will be more golden or brownish, while natural Citrine is more of a pale yellow. A heat-treated stone will need some kind of healing ritual to restore it to its natural energies.

Citrine is a stone for the second or third chakra, depending on its color. It brings in the energy of the Sun and opens our mind to higher thoughts beyond fears and doubts. Citrine gives us the patience and endurance we need to focus our mind on details, such as writing, planning, and putting things in their proper order.

See *Golden Flame* on page A8 for a Citrine piece.

Diamond

MARS ♂, VENUS ♀, MERCURY ☿, SUN ☉, SATURN ♄, URANUS ♅

The Diamond is to me one of the most beautiful stones of all. It has the highest reflection of light and is the hardest and most durable of all gems. It crystallizes in a double pyramid shape as an octahedron.

The Diamond represents the life-force energy of the Sun, the highest expression of light and consciousness in our solar system and therefore serving as the gateway to higher perceptions of reality, other realms and dimensions.

Diamond also represents the Wise King, like King Arthur, so beautifully portrayed in the movie *Excalibur.* King Arthur recovers from his illness with the help of his spiritual adviser and magician, Merlin. He achieves a higher state of consciousness, a state of oneness. This is his healing.

Many of our myths and stories show the individual hero struggling against some challenge; conquering that challenge requires growth and evolution to a higher state of understanding and consciousness. This is the quest that we all pursue. The Diamond is a metaphor for this process: it is mined, cut, and polished, evolving toward a state of ever more refined perfection until it becomes a perfect manifestation of light and wisdom. Does this not mirror our own path toward a greater state of enlightened perfection?

Although there are many other stones that are beautiful and precious in their natural state, it is Diamond that is accorded the place of honor as the most special and precious gemstone. We intuitively appreciate the qualities of the Diamond and elevate it to this status. In the Ayurvedic and East Indian religious traditions, women are discouraged from wearing Diamonds because they are considered too empowering; but I encourage all women to take part in the empowering and consciousness-enhancing qualities of the Diamond!

The Diamond helps us to connect with our creativity and the power radiating out from the center of our being. We mistakenly attribute too much importance to our manifested personality. We must uncover our underlying universal power, wisdom, and radiance, as manifested in our dreams and creativity. Supported by the Diamond, we delve below our outward personality and discover our true selves.

As Diamond is the hardest stone on the Mohs' scale, it supports us by helping us to achieve structure, self-discipline, and endurance in our lives so that we may extend the boundaries of our capacities.

The Diamond represents the crown chakra, our connection to unity consciousness, to all that is. It refracts light prismatically like a rainbow, representing our eternal connection to the divine source.

Given all of these superb qualities, we can all benefit from wearing a Diamond, wherever we are on our path. Its strength is enhanced when it is worn with the right awareness, helping us, through our human consciousness, to discover that we are part of the divine consciousness.

Whenever we wear a Diamond in combination with other colored stones, it enhances the qualities of the colored stone. I love to combine Diamonds with other stones in my jewelry; it's like shining the light of consciousness into specific areas of your life.

Green Diamond
MARS ♂, VENUS ♀, SUN ☉, JUPITER ♃, SATURN ♄

The Green Diamond is a very rare being. The largest and most famous one is the 41-karat Dresden Diamond, purchased by King Frederick Augustus II of Saxony in 1743; it is displayed in the palace in Dresden, Germany.

Many Green Diamonds used in jewelry today are irradiated to achieve their green color. I am hesitant to use radiated stones in my jewelry, but the Green Diamond definitely has powerful capabilities even when treated.

The Green Diamond teaches us about the riches of the heart. It is an androgynous being with both male and female qualities. She is the lover and the beloved. He is the healer of the heart and makes it strong to protect it from hurt—pain may still be experienced, but it stops short of suffering. Balance and nourishment are found in our hearts so that we need little from outside ourselves. The king and queen are married in your own heart. Fulfillment and joy find their expression in everything we do and create in the world.

Our inner abundance is mirrored in outer abundance. Richness and abundance are a state of mind, not a manifestation of possessions. Whenever we are in an abundant state of mind we feel the urge to share our abundance with others and we find that indeed, there is plenty for everyone. Abundance of the heart and spirit and the grace that ensues from them—those are the lessons of Green Diamond.

Yellow Diamond
VENUS ♀, MERCURY ☿, SUN ☉, JUPITER ♃, SATURN ♄

The Yellow Diamond has the highest light reflection of all yellow gemstones. It is a unique and highly coveted stone. The most famous Yellow Diamond is the Florentine Diamond, a huge, 126-facet stone weighing 137.27 carats. Found in India, it first appears in legends in 1467 worn by Charles the Bold, Duke of Burgundy. Since then, it has belonged to the Medici family and a variety of European royalty. It disappeared from the possession of the Austrian imperial family during their World War I exile to Switzerland.

The Yellow Diamond represents the Sun and pure life energy and joy, meaning also love. Its golden light radiates into our body and soul, reminding us of the truth of who we are: eternal beings of light and spirit.

The Yellow Diamond stimulates and enhances our creativity and self-expression. It represents an artist of life who is able to celebrate and respond to life and its challenges. The wearer of the Yellow Diamond can stay very focused, determined, and patient as projects unfold.

This Diamond imparts the ability to keep the bigger picture in mind without getting lost in details, making us very successful in all our endeavors. We become winners with a golden touch, like King Midas. The beauty of the Yellow Diamond is that all this is accomplished from a place of love and sharing of our abilities with the world. The Yellow Diamond models leadership in the new millennium.

The Yellow Diamond is shown in *Spiral Dance* on page A12.

Diopside

JUPITER ♃, SATURN ♄

Diopside usually has a dark bottle-green or emerald-green color and grows in monoclinic[1] columnar crystals. It is found all over the world, including varieties such as Star Diopside and Diopside Cat's Eye.

This friend is at our side in our search for meaning in life, our search for God. Diopside opens our perceptions to new dimensions and insights into the nature of our human existence. It helps us to grow beyond our limiting concepts about ourselves and the world. As we center ourselves within our heart, we become more conscious of what we are looking for and yearning for in life, and we are able to establish new paths that lead us where we want to go.

Diopside will keep us on track toward achieving a larger vision and finding ways to manifest that vision in daily life.

Dioptase

VENUS ♀, MOON ☽, JUPITER ♃

Dioptase is an emerald-green stone with a tinge of blue. It forms short hexagonal crystals. It occurs in Chile, Namibia, and Russia.

Dioptase is a family-oriented being. It connects us with our instinct for tribal affiliation, which expands our field of consciousness. It helps us to choose the right group of friends, people who share our characteris-

....
1 Having three unequal axes, two of which intersect obliquely and are perpendicular to the third.

tics and values. It encourages us to grow beyond ourselves as individuals, to form connections and identify with a greater human network and thus a larger life view.

As a stone for the heart, Dioptase nourishes and refreshes the physical heart and aids recovery after illness or surgery.

Emerald

VENUS ♀, MERCURY ☿, MOON ☽, JUPITER ♃, CHIRON ⚷

The name of the Emerald comes from the Greek word *smaragdos,* meaning "green stone." In ancient times, the word probably referred not only to Emeralds but to most green stones. Its color is so special that the color emerald green is named after it.

Along with Aquamarine, Emerald is the most fashionable, precious, and popular of the Beryls. The most important deposits are in Columbia, especially the Muzo Mine west of Bogota. This stone was already highly valued by the Mayas, whose mines were rediscovered in the seventeenth century.

The Emerald crystallizes in hexagonal prisms which grow in small veins or on the walls of cavities. It has a Mohs' hardness of 7½–8, making it a relatively hard stone. But it is a very brittle stone, sensitive to striking and pressure, and so needs to be treated with care.

Emerald is the queen and high priestess of the Beryl group, wielding both worldly and spiritual power. Being a queen and somewhat fragile, it needs to be treated with respect, but will return to you its manifold gifts.

Emerald shares with you abundant energy, both physical and spiritual. It helps you to expand beyond your fear into higher wisdom, praising and enjoying life. It represents infinite consciousness expressing itself through wisdom and eternal unconditional love.

Emerald is a powerful healer, connecting us with the omnipotent healing strength of God. It provides regeneration in times of convalescence. It helps to connect with our spirit in times of psychic or emotional drain, recharging us with energy and hope. In the Emerald we might find all the nourishment, empowerment, wisdom, and soothing energy we need in difficult times. It centers and calms the mind by balancing the right and the left hemispheres of the brain, raising us up into a higher meditative state of mind.

The Emerald is one of the most feminine representatives of the mineral kingdom: the Shakti, the divine mother, and the goddess. Thus the Emerald is able to teach us what it means to be a powerful woman, how to come into ourselves in all our roles and challenges as women: mother, passionate tantric lover, caring wife, and creative, successful, and fulfilled professional.

In jewelry, I like to combine the Emerald and the Diamond. They are like Shiva and Shakti, Yin and Yang, balancing the highest manifestations of the feminine and masculine principles in the mineral kingdom. Together they carry everything we need to support our growth.

See *Heart Treasure* on page A9 for an Emerald piece.

Garnet

MARS ♂, VENUS ♀, MOON ☽, JUPITER ♃, SATURN ♄

The Garnets are a many-hued family, with different names for each color. The color range includes red, red with a violet tint, reddish brown, orange-brown, yellow, and green. The varieties include Pyrope (reddish brown), Almandine (violet), Spessartite (orange to reddish brown), Grossular (green, yellow, or copper brown), Demantoid (green to emerald green), and Tsavorite (much like emerald green). All of the colors are strongly reflective.

With a relatively high Mohs' hardness of 7–7½, the Garnet makes a nice hard stone for rings and other jewelry. It is found around the world, including in the United States, Sri Lanka, Brazil, Zambia, Tanzania, Afghanistan, India, Brazil, Austria, Germany, and Sweden. Due to its diverse origins this is a very "open-minded" family. It reminds us to welcome and celebrate the diversity of people and their different ways of self-expression.

The Garnet group is very down to earth and practically minded, and thus can assist us in our worldly endeavors and in manifesting our dreams and visions.

Almandine

MARS ♂, VENUS ♀, MERCURY ☿, NEPTUNE ♆

Almandine is a red garnet with a slight violet tint. The form of its crystallization gives it a kind of round crystal ball appearance. If you can find one, it is a nice stone to have in your pocket to play with in order to have the stone's energy within your aura without needing it to be set into jewelry.

Almandine is a warrior of the heart, longing to express his true being as he walks the path of love. Being connected with Venus and Mars, Almandine supports our growth in relationships and friendships. This warrior is connected with the higher truth of the crown chakra: it helps to balance our Inner Man and the Inner Woman, helps us to rise up out of the limitations of the ego to a greater understanding of love as a state of consciousness. It might support us by asking the question, "What can I bring to this relationship?" rather than "What can I get out of it?"

In Almandine, Mars and Venus—the lover and the beloved—are united and re-created on the earthly plane for the pure pleasure of experiencing each other. Almandine encourages us to partake of the enjoyment of love and relationships and to become more conscious of our role in their creation. It gives us deeper insight into the dynamics of relationships as they are projected onto the earthly playground of the cosmos.

Demantoid

MARS ♂, VENUS ♀, MOON ☽, JUPITER ♃

Demantoid is a green Garnet found in the Ural Mountains and is the most valuable variety of Garnet. It is a very brilliant stone with a higher light reflection than even Diamond. Its color, with its yellowish tint, is unique among the green stones and resonates wonderfully with the green sparkles in the Mexican Fire Opals.

Demantoid is sometimes called the "Diamond of the Heart" due to its soothing, nourishing qualities. It invokes the priestess, the artist, the wise woman. Touching on the solar plexus chakra, it stimulates the expression of feelings through art, giving them form and meaning so that the work of art has the power to transform the spectator.

Demantoid and the Fire Opal join forces, becoming allies to help you to move through whatever may be blocking your artistic self-expression and to maintain your creative momentum. The combined support of Demantoid and Fire Opal will overcome the self-doubts that artists sometimes fall prey to. They allow the eternal artist in us to emerge, an artistic self that transcends our usual perceptions of the self. The artist becomes a conduit for creative expression that flows through the self as through hollow bamboo—a sublime experience that leaves the artist feeling grateful and humble.

Containing iron, Demantoid is also an energizer for the heart. It helps us to move through unpleasant feelings by bringing us to experience them deeply, fully, and truthfully. Demantoid's message is this: All feelings, both positive and negative, belong to the essential human experience, and all must be admitted into our heart if we are to discover and fully experience our true essence. When we resist a negative feeling, it grows, clamoring for recognition. If we open ourselves to the feeling, immerse ourselves calmly and courageously in it, the feeling resolves and we find ourselves in a place of peace, happiness, or deeper understanding.

Golden Garnet
MARS ♂, VENUS ♀, SUN ☉, JUPITER ♃

This is my favorite among the golden yellow stones. Affordable larger pieces of this variety are available and can be used as an impressive center stone, as shown in *Celebrating Life* on page A7.

The Golden Garnet is rather opaque and has many occlusions that add character to the stone. (At times, though, the occlusions may cloud the color, so choose carefully.)

The Golden Garnet has a lively and interesting inner life. With its rich color, it brings golden light, representing the highest form of consciousness, into the heart and all the head centers (the three upper chakras). The heart is the seat of our highest capacity for self-love and unconditional love. It brings spontaneous joy and true meaning to our life.

There is a universal, all-consuming longing for love—our music and film industries and much of our literature revolve largely around romance. The experience of love often feels like we are expanding beyond our previous limitations and identity. But where does love come from? Often we have the impression that other people are the source of our love. And yet within each of us there is a great potential for feeling and manifesting love, awaiting our discovery. Golden Garnet helps you tap into that internal well of love, bringing deepest contentment and joy.

Grossular

MARS ♂, VENUS ♀, JUPITER ♃

Grossular occurs in green, yellow, and copper brown. The browns show qualities similar to those of Pyrope and Spessartite. The green Grossular is very similar to the Demantoid, except that it lacks the diamond-like luster of Demantoid. I would always prefer Demantoid because of its strong radiance.

Pyrope

MARS ♂, VENUS ♀, SATURN ♄

The most common color of Pyrope is red with a brownish tint. Because of its reddish color, it is easy to confuse Pyrope with Ruby, Almandine, or Spinel. The more rose-red version is called Rhodolite. This was a very fashionable stone in the eighteenth and nineteenth centuries.

Pyrope represents a strong peasant, connected to nature and Mother Earth, grounded in the physical world. The wearer of Pyrope enjoys life in its abundance and finds sensual pleasure in the world. If you love to work and use your body physically, you will be drawn to Pyrope. This gemstone calls us to the enjoyment of the temple of the body through sexuality.

The qualities of Pyrope are manifested in the artist working with nature—a landscaper, a sculptor working with wood or stone, or an architect building homes.

Spessartite
MARS ♂, VENUS ♀, SATURN ♄

This Garnet is brownish orange. Spessartite has a yellow undercurrent, which connects it not only to the first and second chakras, but also to the third. Spessartite resembles Pyrope in that it grounds us in the physical world, but it brings us to even more intense joy in life and enjoyment of the world.

Earth Spirit on page A7 uses Spessartite.

Tsavorite
VENUS ♀, MERCURY ☿, SUN ☉, JUPITER ♃

Tsavorite is one of the most popular varieties of the green Garnets. It has an emeraldlike green color with a bluish tint and a high degree of reflection.

Tsavorite is the male counterpart of Demantoid. It represents the healer and magician who helps us tune into our heart's desires and needs. When we become aware of those needs, we must confront our beliefs about our self-worth and the love and care that we deserve. By leading us to question the old limiting beliefs ingrained in our personality, Tsavorite helps us to overcome them and transform them into a healthier self-concept. How can we love and cherish others if we are not able to love and cherish our own being? If we are full of self-hatred, how can we be loving?

Healing takes place through awareness of and compassion for our human condition and all the negative conditioning we have undergone while growing up. The first step is to realize that this is merely conditioning and not who we really are. Our personality is simply the result of our life experiences and the decisions and choices we have made as a result of those experiences. When we become aware of that, we begin to see the difference between our self and our personality, which is the first step on our path to freedom.

Our heart's desire is to be free of limiting beliefs and the suffering that results from those beliefs. Tsavorite helps us to accept ourselves as beings with needs. We learn to feel compassion and to accept our vulnerability. It is only from that place of vulnerability that we can be open enough to receive the things we long for most.

Tsavorite is also the king of the forest, reigning over all that grows in the plant kingdom. This is the stone for the gardener with a green thumb. Plants thrive with the right combination of rich soil, water, sunlight, and perhaps pruning. The same holds true for us: we are the gardeners and caretakers of our selves, nurturing our soul and spirit so that they too may thrive. Tsavorite shares with us the joy of expanding and growing into our larger and better selves.

See a Tsavorite in *Brilliant Heart* on page A7.

Herkimer Diamond

MARS ♂, VENUS ♀, MERCURY ☿, MOON ☽,
SUN ☉, PLUTO ♇, SATURN ♄, URANUS ♅

The Herkimer Diamond, found in Herkimer, New York, is a double-terminated[2] rock crystal with such clarity and brilliance that it was named after the most reflective and brilliant stone there is, the Diamond. A handful of Herkimer Diamonds are as dazzling as real Diamonds. The most common material on the Earth, silica, becomes a sparkling little gem in the Herkimer Diamond.

This stone grows in small air pockets in the mother matrix rock material. It starts as a small seed crystal and grows outward from the center. Some collector's pieces are displayed still embedded in a pocket of air in the mother matrix.

This stone is amazing in its beauty, clarity, and perfection. Unlike the Diamond, which must be cut and polished to bring out its beauty, the Herkimer Diamond is perfect in its natural state and requires no cutting or polishing at all. It is untouched by the human hand. I love to make jewelry with both of these beautiful stones and to combine them in the same piece.

The Herkimer Diamond has a very special place among the gems because of its superior qualities. It is worn most beneficially over the

....
2 A crystal with a point at each end that has grown in clay.

heart. Sitting on the heart chakra, which is the middle one of the seven, it balances the whole energetic system. Thus it is able to strengthen our auric field against all kinds of radiation, including electro smog and negative thought projections. We are constantly targeted by radiation in our daily lives, especially in urban areas. It is known that sitting in front of a computer for several hours can lower our white blood cell count, which inevitably impacts our health. The Herkimer Diamond in its perfection and balance between the negative and positive points can balance us out and strengthen our own energy field.

This stone also strengthens our auric field against negative emotional or mental projections. I have made many Herkimer Diamond pendants for people who work in the healing professions to help them stabilize and treat their clients without picking up their imbalances. The more sensitive you are, the more likely you are to pick up on disharmony in your outer field. The Herkimer Diamond is your ally in maintaining your own balance and strength.

This stone also balances the right and left hemispheres of the brain, the creative and logical, the female and the male sides in us. Most of us tend toward one side or the other. The Herkimer Diamond balances us out in the middle between the two. The creative mind and the logical, scientific mind are enhanced by each other's qualities: the creative mind benefits from greater focus and logic and the scientific mind draws on more creative and intuitive resources. The two hemispheres join forces, resulting in inventions and discoveries beyond the known.

The Herkimer Diamond's brilliancy stimulates our inspiration and connection to higher truth and wisdom. Clarity of thought and a peaceful mind are a matter of balance.

The Herkimer Diamond can be worn very beneficially over your heart or as earrings close to the brain. For jewelry, seek the clearest and most perfect crystals. For meditation or even under your pillow, you may choose a larger crystal, which might not be quite as perfect as the smaller ones. The larger stones have inclusions[3] and rainbows that make

....

3 A natural internal imperfection caused by a foreign body (solid, liquid, or gas) within a gemstone that may enhance or detract from its quality.

them very beautiful nonetheless. The Herkimer Diamond is a gift in its perfection and balancing qualities, a visual reminder of God's perfect creation.

Power of the Soul on page A11 features a Herkimer Diamond.

Jade
VENUS ♀, MOON ☽, JUPITER ♃, NEPTUNE ♆

"Jade" is the name used in the jewelry trade for both Jadeite and Nephrite, two green stones that are so similar, they are difficult to distinguish. I will refer to them here as a single stone because they are almost identical in their metaphysical properties.

The most valuable is the Imperial Jade, a translucent emerald-green stone with chrome pigments found in Burma. In ancient times, it was used for knives and instruments as well as carvings for jewelry and religious and ornamental objects. It was known for its toughness and was highly valued in China and pre-Columbian Central America.

Jade is still highly valued in present-day China and is considered an important part of a family's tradition and heritage. Jade carvings, jewelry, and other objects are kept in the family for many years and passed on to the next generation. It is considered a stone that brings healing for all kinds of ailments, financial good fortune, abundance, and spiritual alignment.

Jade has a very soft, shiny, pearly luster when it is polished. There is a feminine quality to it that no other stone has. It is easily carved and shaped, but is still tough and unyielding. Jade represents a lady in her elegance and posture and is very nourishing and supportive. It balances the heart and softens the hard edges and scars of the heart. Lady Jade reminds me of water: soft and caressing but unyielding and so strong in its own way. No rock can withstand the power of water over time; it will be washed round and smooth and finally eroded to powder.

Jade is indeed a very healing stone. The nourishment we feel with Jade comes from a place inside us, from our own being. Our connection with our own spiritual nature allows us to heal the heart of its grief and wounds. Jade helps us to value our own process of growth and transformation and to be compassionate and patient with the tiny steps we are able to take.

Labradorite

MERCURY ☿, MOON ☽, JUPITER ♃, SATURN ♄, URANUS ♅

Labradorite is a Feldspar cousin of Moonstone, but it occurs in stronger, almost metallic colors, more in the range of green, blue, and a touch of yellow. Viewed from the right angle, the reflected colors really sparkle. This stone was originally found in Labrador, Canada. Today it also comes from Newfoundland, Russia, Mexico, and the United States. Labradorite has a Mohs' hardness of 6–6½. It can be used in rings, but if the ring is worn frequently, the stone must be polished occasionally. It also makes beautiful pendants and you can have large stones made into jewelry without spending too much money.

Labradorite is even more closely connected to the subconscious mind and the intuition and wisdom of the heart than Moonstone. It opens up a connection between the heart and the throat chakra and helps you to express your feelings and your own inner truth. We must value our own inner feelings and sense of who we are to be able to express and maintain them. Labradorite helps us to unveil our emotional needs and wants and also our ability to heal and nourish others. Its mysterious depth and beauty show us our own endless potential, waiting to be manifested. It is a wonderful ally for artists and writers to help them tap into the unconscious mind and its treasures.

Lapis Lazuli

MERCURY ☿, JUPITER ♃, SATURN ♄, NEPTUNE ♆

Lapis Lazuli is composed of different minerals and therefore some gem experts consider it to not be a mineral, but a rock with Lazurite as its main ingredient. This opaque blue stone is not very hard—its Mohs' hardness is only 5–6, making it easy to carve and cut. For that reason, it has been used in jewelry since ancient times. In Egypt, it was considered a sacred stone and was used in jewelry and sacred objects like scarabs. To me, the most beautiful Lapis is dark blue with spots of golden pyrite, which makes it a very unique-looking specimen. Lapis should be set in gold.

The best and darkest quality Lapis Lazuli is found in Afghanistan. Deposits in Chile and Russia yield lighter blue stones with whitish or grayish veins. Lapis Lazuli is a Mercurial stone. Mercury is the messenger of the gods, bringing the fire of consciousness and deepened awareness. He touches the third eye to awaken us to our deep inner nature and truth. Lapis helps us focus our mind, to concentrate and learn. It is a great ally for students, especially during exams, as it enhances our memory. It also connects us to the collective unconscious and strengthens our ability to achieve sudden insights. The brain is like a radio receiver: when it is tuned into a specific station it receives only that station. Lapis helps us tune into the right station, which enhances our memory and connects us to our deeper source of objective knowing.

Lapis brings us peace of mind. In a relaxed state of mind, we develop a realistic and compassionate acceptance of things as they are. While most blue gemstones used in jewelry are translucent, Lapis is opaque, a quality that helps us achieve a concrete problem-solving orientation, supporting a very practical mind that focuses on the task at hand and deals with it, rather than being distracted by extraneous worries.

See *Castle in the Cloud* on page A7 for an example of Lapis Lazuli jewelry.

Moonstone
VENUS ♀, MERCURY ☿, MOON ☽, URANUS ♅, NEPTUNE ♆

The Moonstone, like its cousin Labradorite, belongs to the Feldspar group. Many of the best Moonstones are white with a bluish glow; those are found in Sri Lanka, Burma, Brazil, Australia, and India. The rarest and most valuable, though, is the Rainbow Moonstone, which contains a whole rainbow of colors. It is found only in India. The Moonstone also occurs in orange and gray-black stones with a sheen.

I am fascinated by the Rainbow Moonstone and its qualities. This stone represents the high priestess from Avalon, the carrier and teacher of mysteries, the caring sister and the nourishing mother. The Rainbow Moonstone nourishes and balances the emotional system. It soothes our hurts and wounds. Its mysterious beauty speaks to our unconscious. It transmits peace and connects us with the eternal wisdom of the heart and with the essence of who we are. It connects us with our feminine side, a receptive state rather than constant action: it can help us reconnect with a state of "nondoing." This is a place that is nurtured by our soul and guides us toward wisdom and the unfolding of our highest capacities and resources.

We cannot "do" the things that are most important in life: we can strive for what we think is right action, but we cannot make it happen. When I look back over my life, I see that the most important events and turning points were not things that I had any control over. I have tried hard to control and to act, but in the end how my life unfolded wasn't really in my hands; my life was directed by grace or guidance in action. The Rainbow Moonstone helps us to relax into that guidance and have faith in the grace operating in our life. It teaches us about the journey of life, which is not a problem but a mystery to be lived.

The Moonstone is a wonderful companion for our male friends, husbands, and lovers. It brings to males an element of the female spirit and helps them to connect more with their feelings without fearing them. It gives the warrior a heart with gentle feelings. Give the man in your life a big chunk of stone to carry in his pocket or to wear as a pendant over his heart.

Magic Flows on page A9 is a Moonstone piece.

Opal

MARS ♂, VENUS ♀, MERCURY ☿, MOON ☽,
PLUTO ♇, SATURN ♄, URANUS ♅, NEPTUNE ♆

The Opal family is divided into three groups: the opalescent precious Opals, the yellow-red Fire Opals, and the common Opals. The first two are characterized by their opalescence, a rainbowlike sparkling and iridescence that changes when viewed from different angles. It might be found as Opal Matrix, embedded in the matrix rock material it has grown in. Each gem is individual and unique, but this is especially true in the world of the Opals—there are no two Opals alike. If you fall in love with one while shopping, buy it because you will never find the same one again. Opal is sensitive to pressure and knocks and will be affected by acids and alkalis.

Australia is the primary source of the best quality Opals. They are also found in Brazil, Guatemala, Honduras, Japan, and the United States.

Opal has no crystal structure; it is amorphous. Its molecules are layered in a siliceous[4] jelly and it can contain up to 30 percent water. This water is essential to the stone: if it loses water, it may crack, the color may change, or the opalescence may diminish. It is always good to moisten the stone, especially when stored away for a time. In my observation, because of its very liquid composition, the stone's colors vary significantly with the emotional status of the wearer. So, no, it's not your imagination if your stone changes its color from day to day!

Black Opal

MARS ♂, PLUTO ♇, SATURN ♄, URANUS ♅, NEPTUNE ♆

The Black Opal is a precious Opal in the color range of dark gray, dark blue, dark green, red, or gray-black. It has qualities similar to those of Boulder Opal and Opal Matrix and leans toward the energy of Neptune, deepening our intuitive knowledge of who we are and the experience of feeling connected and held by the creator of the universe.

See page A7 for *Divine Waters*, a Black Opal piece.

....
4 Having a high silica content.

Boulder Opal and Opal Matrix

VENUS ♀, MERCURY ☿, PLUTO ♇, SATURN ♄, URANUS ♅,
NEPTUNE ♆

The Boulder Opal is primarily found in Queensland, Australia. This precious, colorful stone is found layered in cracks and crevices in ironstone and sandstone boulders. The Boulder Opal forms on a backing of ironstone, which gives it strength. It is famous worldwide for its vibrant colors, stability, strength, and uniqueness. In Opal Matrix, the ironstone or sandstone might show at the surface and create very unusual designs and structures mixed in with the colors.

These Opals come in all kinds of sparkling colors, including green, blue, turquoise, yellow, red, and violet in a wide variety of combinations and shades.

The precious Opal is always a mixture of all the energies of the outer planets. The color of the stone determines the planetary principle that it represents: the dark blues lean more toward Pluto and the green-blue-turquoises toward Uranus, while the very colorful Opals and the Black Opals express the energy of Neptune.

Because of their connection with the matrix rock, the transforming energies of the Boulder Opal or Opal Matrix are very grounding and essential for us. They help us to stay rooted and grounded during times of upheaval in our lives—those times when we might otherwise lose faith and not know how to stay centered.

Matrix means "mother." The ironstone matrix holds the colorful veins of the Opal together, giving the stone a solid structure—a holding environment and something to rely on, just as we relied on our mothers in childhood.

Opal is the stone of the mystic, shaman, artist, and healer in all of us. It is a stone for support during times of transition and intense change.

Opals in the blue-violet-turquoise color range work with the throat chakra and the third eye. This Opal gives us a more holistic view of things and helps us to let go of old mental "garbage"—thoughts, memories, and issues that may be blocking our present thriving. In order to engage in a process of positive change, we must learn to change old limiting beliefs and mental patterns. Change starts in the mind, in the way we are able to see ourselves and the world around us. If we are ready and willing to change, our transits with the outer planets, marking major challenges and transitions, will be easier.

The Opal also stimulates our creativity and our search for meaning and vision in life—qualities that help to ease our transitions through periods of challenge.

The green-blue variety gives us more understanding in working with the heart and the throat chakras. This stone is particularly suited to helping us overcome old wounds that prevent us from being open to the emotional fulfillment we long for. This Opal will help heal the heart, bringing awareness of our true feelings and helping us learn to express our personal truth from the heart.

All Opals need to be handled with care. They are sensitive to knocks and pressure and don't like acids or alkalis. You should remove Opal jewelry before doing jobs such as gardening or painting your house.

See a Boulder Opal in *Ocean Spirit* on page A10.

Crystal Clear Fire Opal
MOON ☽, PLUTO ♇, URANUS ♅, NEPTUNE ♆

This is the female Fire Opal: transcendent, brilliant, sparkling in many hues. This Opal is like a drop of water radiating shining colors from its depths.

The Crystal Clear Fire Opal represents the Amazon woman, strong and independent. She never gives her power away to her mate. She is a friend, lover, and companion. She values her sisters highly as a source of support, wisdom, and nourishment.

This stone connects us to the collective unconscious and all the treasures it enfolds. It fuels our intuition with sudden sparks of insight and wisdom. But it is also the universal mother guiding and nourishing us, sustaining us in times of trouble and difficulties. It helps us in times of change to keep our courage and to transform ourselves. Accompanied by the Crystal Clear Fire Opal, a woman who has grown and transformed herself through challenge and difficulty becomes more real and in touch with her true being.

Free Spirit on page A8 is a nice Crystal Clear Fire Opal piece.

Fire Opal
MARS ♂, VENUS ♀, PLUTO ♇, NEPTUNE ♆

The Fire Opal, found primarily in Mexico, gets its name from its orange color. It can be milky or, in the best quality stones, clear and transparent. A very good quality stone exhibits a high degree of green-red opalescence. The most colorful and interesting stones are the matrix specimens.

The Fire Opal is the master of the energizing stones. It represents the warrior expanding his territory in any direction he chooses. When our movement in a particular direction is long overdue, the Fire Opal imparts its fire to us to get us moving. The wearer of this gem is an adventurer, a pioneer, someone who loves to discover new lands. The Fire Opal can encourage us in times of drastic changes and transformation. It can give us extra energy and motivation for mastering and feeling more comfortable in our physical body. It rules the intestinal system and helps our digestion. It gives us energy and flexibility when we are feeling sluggish.

The Fire Opal also represents a Don Juan and a tantric master who loves playful sexuality, radiating enjoyment of the physical senses and helping us to move beyond the physical qualities of that experience. This stone opens us up to real intimacy, because we feel full and strong and centered in our own abdominal center. We can enjoy dissolving and melting with one another without losing ourselves. The Fire Opal opens up new dimensions in our lovemaking.

The Fire Opal relieves tensions in the first three chakras and opens any blockages we may have there. This is a great stone for a belly chain, so you can wear it hanging loose in front of the power center—the *Dan Tien*, as the Chinese call it, meaning "best place in the body."

But Fire Opal is not only very powerful, it is also very gentle and healing in its transmission of energy. It can offer support during recov-

Alexandrite
page 94

Alexandrite
page 94

Amber
page 94

Amethyst
page 95

Amethyst
page 95

Aquamarine
page 98

Aquamarine
page 98

Azurite
page 100

Beryl, Goshenite
page 102

Beryl, Heliodor
page 102

Bloodstone
page 104

Carnelian
page 104

Chrysocolla
page 105

Chrysoprase
page 106

Citrine
page 106

Emerald
page 111

Garnet
page 112

Garnet, Pyrope
page 115

Garnet, Pyrope
page 115

Garnet, Spessarite
page 116

Jade
page 119

Labradorite
page 120

Lapis Lazuli
page 120

Lapis Lazuli
page 120

Moonstone
page 121

Opal
page 123

Opal, Fire
page 126

Peridot
page 129

Peridot
page 129

Quartz
page 130

Ruby
page 132

Ruby
page 132

Ruby, Star
page 133

Sapphire
page 133

Sapphire, Blue
page 135

Sapphire, Yellow
page 138

Tanzanite
page 139

Tourmaline
page 140

Tourmaline, Indigolite
page 141

Tourmaline, Paraiba
page 141

Tourmaline, Rubellite
page 142

Tourmaline, Rubellite
page 142

Tourmaline, Watermelon
page 143

Zircon
page 143

Brilliant Heart
page 117

Castle in the Clouds
page 121

Celebrating Life
page 114

Divine Intervention
page 171

Divine Love
page 96

Divine Waters
page 123

Earth Spirit
page 116

Evolution
page 139

Expanding Heart
page 83

Free Spirit
page 126

Full Heart
page 130

Golden Flame
page 107

Golden True Love
page 138

Grace Upon Us
page 142

Heart Treasure
page 112

Infinite Balance
page 129

Integration
page 133

Life Weaves a Pattern
page 137

Limitless Sky
page 135

Magic Flows
page 122

Merlin's Magic
page 140

Milky Way
page 170

Mother Earth &
Father Sky
page 82

Mountain Dream
page 104

Nature's Balm
page 141

Ocean Spirit
page 125

One Spirit
page 136

Open Heart
page 105

Peace Finder
page 127

Power of the Soul
page 119

Precious Jewels
page 168

Queens Pearl
page 129

Royal Fire
page 128

Show Me My Destiny
page 171

Sky & Ocean
page 100

Spiral Dance
page 110

Sweet Love
page 129

Touched by an Angel
page 135

Touched by Grace
page 133

True Heart
page 143

Waves
page 137

ery from sexual abuse. It helps us to rise out of conceiving of ourselves as victims, helps us to develop forgiveness, and empowers us by releasing those toxic thoughts from our system. It bolsters our sense of personal power and mastery.

I love this stone and use it in many different combinations in my jewelry: with the Demantoid for artistic guidance, with the Diamond for radical empowerment and breaking through barriers, and with the Moonstone for balancing Yin and Yang energies and active and passive qualities.

A Fire Opal can be seen in *Expanding Heart* on page A8.

Lightning Ridge Opal
MERCURY ☿, PLUTO ♇, SATURN ♄, URANUS ♅, NEPTUNE ♆

The town of Lightning Ridge in New South Wales, Australia, yields some of the most striking Opals in the world, famous for their exceptional color and brilliance. These are Black and Crystal Opals that occur in a beautiful deep blue and other color combinations. The name "Lightning Ridge" gives these stones a clear edge in quality and price over other origins. The most desirable and expensive Opals are those with the strongest, most sparkling colors and the most interesting color formations and combinations. Lightning Ridge is the seal of quality in the world of Opals.

See *Peace Finder* on page A11 for a Lightning Ridge Opal.

White Opal
MOON ☽, PLUTO ♇, URANUS ♅, NEPTUNE ♆

White Opals occur in more white or light-based colors. They bring in the transformative and refining energies of the outer planets along with the soothing Moon qualities, making us feel nourished, balanced, and in touch with our feelings. The White Opal represents the Lady of the Lake who invites us to embark on an inner journey, diving down into the depths of our being, the depths of the ocean of the unconscious, to find unknown and unimaginable treasures to bring up with us into the world above. Being renewed, rejuvenated, and deeply changed as a result of this journey, we have a new outlook on life.

White Opal appears in *Royal Fire* on page A11.

Pearl

MOON ☽, SATURN ♄, NEPTUNE ♆, CHIRON ⚷

Pearls are found in a great variety of colors, including white, cream, rose, silver, gold, blue, and black. Pearl is an organic substance made of calcium carbonate and an organic horn material that forms as a reaction to an injury to an oyster's mantle folds, usually intentionally caused by humans. The Pearl forms concentrically around the implanted microcrystal. Pearls are very sensitive to acids, perspiration, cosmetics, hairspray, dryness, and humidity. They can die through age or improper treatment, or they can become dull, crack, and peel.

Pearls are sometimes referred to as the "tears of the soul" and some advise against wearing them. There may well be some truth in that notion, but the choice to wear pearls must be left to individual discretion: I feel a strong attraction toward some pearls and appreciate wearing them frequently.

The Pearl can be viewed as a being originating in the depths of the ocean or fresh water seas. Water or the ocean is a powerful symbol and representation of our unconscious mind, the unknown depths of our emotions, the female part of our being. The human body consists of 85 percent water, the mysterious ingredient essential to all life. And science tells us that we normally use only 5 to 10 percent of the potential of our brains, the conscious mind, meaning that the majority of the brain is hidden in the vast unconscious. The significance of the Pearl's association with deep waters, and therefore our unconscious mind, is clear!

The Moon rules water, the ocean, the emotions, the female principle, and our unconscious mind. The Pearl is ruled by the Moon, so it connects us with the depths of our unconscious and our feelings, including those that we often seek to repress, such as grief, sorrow, and pain. We try to avoid becoming conscious of those wounds, but we should take a lesson from the Pearl: Pearl's host, the shell, also suffered an injury—even died at one point!—and yet produced this perfect, soft, shiny, round beauty.

The transformation is reminiscent of the caterpillar, often ugly, that grows into a beautiful butterfly. And so is it with humans: we can use our wounds like the Pearl, to grow into our own magnificent beauty.

Having this "wound" affinity with humans, Pearl is a wonderful ally and friend to us during our process of healing from these deep emotional injuries. It can soothe and nourish us, bring our wounds up into the light of consciousness, and assist us in the transforming healing process.

The round shape of the Pearl, the most balanced form there is, stands for perfection and oneness.

See *Sweet Love* on page A12 and *Queens Pearl* on page A11 for beautiful Pearl jewelry pieces.

Black Pearl

MOON ☽, SATURN ♄, NEPTUNE ♆, CHIRON ⚷

The Black Pearl, also called Tahitian Pearl, is cultivated in the ocean and has many qualities of Saturn. This makes it the deepest and most intense of the Pearl sisters. Thus it teaches us compassion and self-love. It makes us aware of the limits we create for ourselves, of the armor we put on in our attempt to shield ourselves from further hurts, of loneliness and aloneness, and of our deep commitment to life and all the inevitable changes that life entails.

Infinite Balance on page A9 features Black Pearl.

Peridot

VENUS ♀, SUN ☉, JUPITER ♃

The Peridot, sometimes called Olivine, has a unique gold-green color. It is found in numerous places in the world, including St. John's Island, Egypt; Australia; Brazil; Hawaii; and New Mexico. It is not a very hard stone, rating 6½–7 on the Mohs' scale. If you wear it in a ring, you need to be very careful with it.

The Peridot represents a very feminine lady—Venus and Isis in one of her disguises, ruling and nourishing the heart. It taps into the joy of living and caring and sharing. Art can be an expression of love that nourishes the soul and heart, and the Peridot is the patroness of artists and lovers. There is a generosity to a full heart, a loving glow that the heart wants to find a way to express. The Peridot connects the solar plexus chakra and the heart chakra and expands our creative self-expression in alignment with the heart.

The aptly named *Full Heart* on page A8 contains Peridot.

Quartz, or Rock Crystal
MERCURY ☿, SUN ☉, SATURN ♄, CHIRON ⚷

Crystal Quartz is one of the most common and well-known crystals in the world, found virtually everywhere on the planet. It is composed of silicon dioxide and forms six-sided hexagonal prisms.

The word *crystal* derives from the Greek *krystallos,* meaning "ice," as the Greeks believed that Quartz was water that was eternally frozen, an image also found in the work of Hildegard von Bingen, a saint and ancient seer of the healing aspects of stones. Ice is a metaphor for the cooling and clear aspects of the crystal.

Quartz is a very sociable being, growing in groups and clusters and very often found together or in close connection with other minerals; thus it teaches us to have close, friendly relationships without losing our individuality and center.

Like the Diamond, Quartz is very closely connected to our search for light and love, our longing to awaken to a higher state of consciousness, and it is our guide on that quest.

Crystal Quartz is the manifestation of light, clarity, concentration, and perfect crystallization, a metaphor for our own search for perfection. If you examine a single crystal you will see that as it grows it becomes more and more clearly developed and defined toward the tip. You can also see the six sides of the crystal, corresponding to the first six chakras in the body, with the tip of the crystal corresponding to the crown chakra. In this way, Quartz is a perfect mirror for our process of growth as we move from confused or unenlightened to a state of increasing awareness and clarity on our path to higher consciousness.

Quartz is a good friend, brother, and sister and may have many additional properties, depending on the form of its "face," or crystal tip. It might enhance our psychic abilities, such as channeling, telepathy, and clairvoyance, or connecting us with ancient teachings and spiritual knowledge. I have had several interesting experiences with a crystal that has small triangles as if engraved in the facets of its tip, as an opener to the past life experiences of Atlantis. Such a crystal might work like a computer chip, carrying information to be read. Isn't it interesting that both Quartz and computer chips are made from silicon dioxide?

Although every stone may be said to pick up information by absorbing vibrations, Quartz is especially sensitive to the environment, absorbing everything around it. So it is very important to program it to do this consciously and to clean it often. This cleaning can be done with the help of all the elements and with the conscious state of your mind in combination with rapid, strong exhalations.

A double-terminated crystal (one with two tips on each end) sets up an energy flow between the two ends, which act as positive and negative electromagnetic poles, and thus is especially adept at balancing opposites like Yin and Yang. In a single-pointed crystal, the energy rises up from the more clouded bottom toward the clear tip.

A crystal in a spherical form—a crystal ball—gives off a wide, radiant, harmonizing energy field that, depending on the size of the crystal, can fill a whole room with sparkles of light and awareness. Because the sphere is the most perfect form in the universe, it brings out its being in the highest form. By directing your thoughts to influence the energies of the crystal, you might program it with your needs and create a very powerful energy field for healing, concentration, or whatever you long for. If you want to deepen your knowledge of the world of Quartz crystals, you may consult the remarkable works of Katrina Raphael.[5]

....

5 Including her three-volume *Crystal Enlightenment: The Transforming Properties of Crystals and Healing Stones* (Aurora Press, 1985).

Ruby

MARS ♂, VENUS ♀, SUN ☉, NEPTUNE ♆

The Ruby is named for the Latin word for its red color, *rubens*. The Ruby has been known to gemologists since the 1800s, when it was first distinguished from its red cousins Spinel and Garnet.

Along with the Sapphires, the Ruby is a member of the Corundum group. It is the second hardest stone after the Diamond, with a hardness of 9 on the Mohs' Scale, making it a very solid stone when set in a ring. It grows and crystallizes in a hexagonal structure.

Inclusions are common in Rubies and sometimes indicate where the stone originated. Layering of rutile needles[6] can produce a soft sheen or even a six-rayed star on a cabochon stone.

The most expensive Ruby color is pure red with a tint of blue called "pigeon's blood." A good quality Ruby can be more expensive than a Diamond. Each stone is one of a kind, which adds to its value.

The Ruby is the warrior of the heart, the knight of our dreams. It touches the root chakra and the heart chakra, helping to gently but powerfully bring energy up from the root chakra to the heart. The root chakra is our connection with the Earth, our grounding, ego identity, survival instincts, anger, sex drive, and life force in general. The heart chakra is the seat of our emotions of love in all its aspects, from self-love to unconditional love. It is the site of unresolved wounds suffered in love and childhood experiences—but it is also home to forgiveness and compassion.

The Ruby is a stone for lovers and their subtler sexual energies. The whole arena of tantric love belongs to Ruby. The wearer of Ruby loves to play and enjoy the physical senses in all their variations and possibilities. He is the king charming the queen, laying his kingdom at her feet.

In this respect, the Ruby is the creator of dreams, the pursuer of the impossible. Unlimited creativity is at Ruby's command, ready to flow into any enterprise.

....

6 Rutile is a mineral composed of titanium dioxide. It forms fine lines, or needles, in "star" gems such as Sapphires and Rubies.

In stimulating the upward flow of our life force, the Ruby is the catalyst of our evolution, leading us to grow beyond our ego fixations and animal drives and to develop the potentials of the realm of the heart. We are all engaged in this grand journey throughout our lifetimes; the Ruby lends us a gentle hand of encouragement along the way.

The Ruby is beautiful in a ring or in a pendant worn over the heart, reflecting its connection with the heart. See *Integration* on page A9 for a Ruby pendant.

Star Ruby

MARS ♂, VENUS ♀, SUN ☉, NEPTUNE ♆

In the shape of a cabochon stone, the Ruby may have a six-sided star moving and reflecting light over its surface, resulting in a special variation on the qualities described above. The Star Ruby represents Venus and Mars in communion, their heart, body, and soul joined in the bedroom. Although from two different stars, they're happily united. There is a healing balance between the male and female principles.

Is not this balance, acceptance, and support of our many aspects what we all long for, both within and with our partner? The Ruby teaches the respect and support that are the necessary ingredients of a successful relationship.

Touched by Grace on page A12 features Star Ruby.

Sapphire

MARS ♂, VENUS ♀, MERCURY ☿, JUPITER ♃, SATURN ♄

The name "Sapphire" comes from the Greek word for "blue." The Sapphire belongs to the Corundum family. The red variety is called Ruby and all other color variations are called Sapphire. There are black, pink, violet, green, yellow, and orange Sapphires. The orange variety is also called Padparadscha, which means "Lotus flower" in Sinhalese, the language of Sri Lanka. Sapphires are found in many places around the world, with the best qualities coming from Australia, Sri Lanka, Burma, Thailand, Kashmir, and Montana.

With a hardness of 9 on the Mohs' scale, the Sapphire is the second hardest stone after the Diamond, making it a very durable stone and excellent for wedding bands and a lifetime of wear.

Besides the Tourmaline, the Sapphire is the only stone that occurs in all the colors of the rainbow. Each color touches us in a different way. Sapphires are especially powerful if different colors are set together in a piece of jewelry.

The rainbow symbolizes beauty and the treasure waiting for us at its end. Discovering that treasure always involves a journey. At some point in our journey, we might realize that the journey itself is the goal. The journey is always happening in the now, and the now is all there is. The beautiful family of the Sapphires can help us to live in the now, to enjoy ourselves as we are, to make peace with ourselves and our life.

Black Star Sapphire

MARS ♂, VENUS ♀, PLUTO ♀, SATURN ♄

This Sapphire has a six-rayed star of reflected light moving around its cabochon surface. The star represents Venus and Mars united, holding hands.

This Sapphire is a strong ally and teacher. His fortes are discipline, endurance, and balance in all extremes and opposing energies. Mars and Venus are the female and the male principles, the lover and the beloved, the Yin and Yang. The Black Star Sapphire grounds those energies in us, giving us peace and deep relaxation.

The Black Sapphire is one of the most powerful among the black stones, a powerful magician. Working with the power of magnetic attraction, Black Sapphire helps us achieve the open-minded receptivity that makes things fall into place easily. This is a wish-fulfilling gem. With its help, we learn to become clear, focused, and receptive to the fulfillment of our goals.

Blue Sapphire

MARS ♂, VENUS ♀, MERCURY ☿, JUPITER ♃, SATURN ♄,
URANUS ♅

The Blue Sapphire varies from light blue to dark blue. The most expensive color is cornflower blue. The coloring pigments are iron (Mars) and titanium (Uranus).

The Blue Sapphire brings us peace of mind. It helps to relax anxiety-driven thoughts by helping us to look at situations from a higher perspective. It helps us to find meaning in the situation we are dealing with and to gain faith in the goodness of life.

If we can live our days from a place of trust in life, that everything is happening for a reason and is part of a bigger plan even if we cannot see it, we find peace. We can relax by putting our fears and worries in the hands of that Higher Force, whatever you choose to call it.

The Blue Sapphire also strengthens and grounds us in our activities. It is responsible and reliable and helps us to follow through on our commitments. It gives us the virtue of patience.

You may also find a Star Sapphire, which is a very special treasure with the integrating love of Venus, the feminine. Star Sapphires include a star-shaped pattern called an asterism.

Though we are firmly grounded on the Earth, the Blue Sapphire soars with us into the unlimited heavens, opening us to higher insight, vision, and wisdom. Innovation and inventions may flow from this new position: it is a place of revolutionary ideas and higher ideals. Best of all, the Blue Sapphire has sufficient energy to make sure we act on those new thought forms, bringing them to life.

The Blue Sapphire is a male stone at its best. It is a healer and mentor for our active mind.

Touched by an Angel on page A12 and *Limitless Sky* on page A9 are two examples of Blue Sapphire rings.

Green Sapphire

MARS ♂, VENUS ♀, JUPITER ♃, SATURN ♄

The color of the Green Sapphire is imparted by iron pigments. This is a stone for matters of the heart. It helps us to listen to the wisdom of the heart, to find our comfortable internal home, and to become aware of the grace that resides there and is always available to us.

In looking back over my life, I am able to see that in spite of all the hard moments that I, like everyone, have experienced, grace has always been present in my life. It has influenced my path at specific junctions or turning points, providing me with just the help I needed at those moments. In spite of my many personal limitations, I gratefully acknowledge the many small and large miracles that have brought me beyond those limitations to where I am today: this is the presence of grace in our lives. The Green Sapphire reminds us that we are securely held by grace at all times.

See a Green Sapphire in *One Spirit* on page A10.

Orange-Pink Sapphire

VENUS ♀, MERCURY ☿, SUN ☉, JUPITER ♃

Also called the Padparadscha, this is a rarer and more expensive Sapphire. This very beautiful radiant stone combines the qualities of the Pink and Yellow Sapphires in one stone. Because it touches the solar plexus and the heart chakras, it especially helps us to express our creative flow in accordance with the heart. The value of an action is measured by the virtues of the heart: unconditional love, self-love, and compassion. We are asked to align our deeds with the heart, which gives us a deep sense of fulfillment and love for our work.

The Orange-Pink Sapphire represents the wise King Arthur ruling with love and integrity. It helps us to share a joyful presence and connection to our higher being, which results in divine right action.

Pink Sapphire

VENUS ♀, JUPITER ♃, NEPTUNE ♆

The Pink Sapphire is very similar to the Ruby in appearance, chemical composition, and vibrational frequency. Only its lighter color distinguishes it from the Ruby.

In general, the Pink Sapphire presents a gentler version of the qualities of the Ruby. It emphasizes the heart a little more and supports self-love. It connects us with the sweetness of life, unconditional mother's love, making us feel safe and content. When we experience the love we long for, all is right with the world, nothing is missing.

Life Weaves a Pattern on page A9 is a Pink Sapphire example.

Violet Sapphire

VENUS ♀, MERCURY ☿, JUPITER ♃, NEPTUNE ♆

The color of the Violet Sapphire and its unusually high vibrational frequency come from Vanadium, a soft and ductile gray-white metal.

The Violet Sapphire assists us in our meditation, helping us to connect with our supreme being to enter a higher state of consciousness. This stone satisfies our longing for the divine. It radiates a crisp, clear energy that cuts through what is peripheral and unimportant to connect us with our own inner wisdom and objective knowing. This wisdom is different from the accumulation of academic knowledge; what I am referring to is a deep intuitive knowledge of truth that does not require external validation. It may be called our connection to the collective unconscious or the morphogenetic field.[7] The Violet Sapphire taps into that field and makes us more aware of it.

The Violet Sapphire tunes our antenna into that deep internal wisdom and aids the flow of inspiration into our conscious mind so we can use it for our creative endeavors. This is the Divine Fool moving with the dance of life and enjoying every step of it.

Waves on page A12 features Violet Sapphire.

....

7 The biological field holding all the information needed to form a living being.

Yellow Sapphire

VENUS ♀, MERCURY ☿, SUN ☉, JUPITER ♃

The Yellow Sapphire is a wonderful friend to accompany us on our journey through life—full of abundant, joyful, creative energy. Its golden yellow color radiates to our solar plexus, making it softer and more relaxed. This is where all our fears and anxieties can be felt—sometimes if we really tune in these can be felt as "butterflies" in the belly. All these exciting energies are swirling around there, seeking a way to be expressed. The Yellow Sapphire is the Sun in our power center, stimulating our powers of self-expression and creativity in all that we do.

The Sun nourishes our body and soul with pure life force. Everyone loves to lie in the sunlight and receive that energy. We know that the Sun stimulates glandular production and has been used to cure many different diseases throughout the ages. Sunlight helps also with depression, which many people experience through a long hard winter with overcast days.

The Yellow Sapphire connects with our nervous system, where it is like a balm, balancing it and equipping it to deal with stress and challenges in a new way. We come up with new ways of looking at problems, dealing with them one step at a time. The Yellow Sapphire sharpens our attention to details and gives us energy to work things out.

The Yellow Sapphire is a wonderful companion for people in the healing professions as it helps to replenish our own energy resources and balance. That is so important for people who are caring for others physically or emotionally. Some research suggests that those in the medical and healing fields have higher than average suicide rates; thus it is crucial for them to restore balance in their systems.

We often pick up lower-frequency energies from our environment and those around us, which makes us ill. Along with the Yellow Sapphire, another stone that shields us from those energies and strengthens and balances our own auric field is the Herkimer Diamond. See above for more information.

Golden True Love on page A8 shows the Yellow Sapphire.

Spinel

MARS ♂, VENUS ♀, SUN ☉, NEPTUNE Ψ

The Spinel, found mainly in Burma and Sri Lanka, looks much like a Ruby. Historically, many stones that were thought to be Rubies have proven to be Spinels. With a Mohs' hardness of 8, it is not as hard as the Ruby and its chemical composition is a little different, with magnesium added to the aluminum oxide. Most Spinels that you will find in the marketplace are red, but they also occur in yellow and blue.

The Spinel is our Lady of the Heart. The wearer of the Spinel is proud, independent, and self-sufficient. She is an artist who expresses herself in many different ways. As the queen beside the king, the Spinel complements the Ruby in his male power.

The Spinel teaches us unconditional love and the beauty of an open heart with no need for armor. It helps to heal emotional trauma while connecting us with the deeper truth of our eternal being. If we are able to get in touch with our true nature as beings of love and perfection, we can achieve a new perspective on difficult life events and find forgiveness in our heart. This will create peace and harmony in our heart and soul. The Spinel gives generously of itself from its heart.

The wearer of the Spinel is also strong and dares to live life according to her own truth and conscience. She is a role model for young girls and helps them to find their own strength as they grow up. They learn to stand out among their peers and discover their potential as leaders rather than followers.

See Spinel in *Evolution* on page A8.

Tanzanite

MERCURY ♀, JUPITER ♃, SATURN ♄, NEPTUNE Ψ

Tanzanite is a very unique blue-violet stone. Found in Tanzania, this stone has only been available on the market for the past thirty years. In artificial light, its color may look more violet than in daylight. It may resemble Blue Sapphire or Amethyst, but Tanzanite is an individual in its own right. It has a Mohs' hardness of 6½–7, a little less hard than

Amethyst. Tanzanite is clear yet soft in appearance. It makes a wonderful stone for jewelry and is even set in rings, but it should be worn with care—I wouldn't leave it on while gardening, for example.

Tanzanite represents Merlin, the spiritual guide and teacher. It encourages us to find our own truth, but to be open to the emergence of a new truth and a higher consciousness. It leads us on a joyous search for deeper meaning and understanding in life, responding to our longing to be rooted in the moment. It stimulates our spiritual search for the divine. It helps us to see and experience our own beauty and spiritual essence. It is truly a guide for all humankind as we begin the new millennium and undertake the next step of our evolution.

Each one of us has a part to play in making this Earth a better place to live, contributing to the morphogenetic field of consciousness in our own way. Tanzanite is our personal guide on the quest for higher consciousness and growth, which is our ultimate contribution.

Tanzanite can be seen in *Merlin's Magic* on page A9.

Tourmaline

MARS ♂, VENUS ♀, MERCURY ☿, JUPITER ♃, NEPTUNE ♆

Tourmaline is a large family of beautiful stones that occur in every color of the rainbow and many different combinations of two-colored stones: green-pink (Watermelon), pink-blue, gold-green, and green-blue, for example. Each color has its own name, but often they are simply called by their color, such as pink Tourmaline (Rubellite), blue Tourmaline (Indigolite), and green-pink Tourmaline (Watermelon Tourmaline). Tourmalines are available as facetted or cabochon stones, with some of the cabochons displaying a cat's eye.

Today most Tourmalines come from Brazil, Sri Lanka, Angola, Australia, Burma, India, Thailand, and the United States (California, New York, Connecticut, and Colorado).

This is a fairly hard stone with a Mohs' hardness of 7–7½. It has a hexagonal crystal structure; the rough crystal wand (a long spike) may be used in jewelry without polishing or cutting because of its natural beauty. Cut slices of a crystal wand come in beautiful and unique color combinations. These make especially nice pendants and earrings.

One of the unique properties of Tourmaline is its piezoelectrical charge: when the crystal is heated or put under pressure, it becomes electrically charged, giving it the ability to attract dust or small bits of paper. Due to this property it was at one time imported to Holland and called *aschentrekker* (ash puller), and was used to pull the ashes out of meerschaum smoking pipes.

Because of this piezoelectric quality, the Tourmaline is the best stone for our nervous system. It acts on the electrical flow within the body, balancing it and restoring the mind-body system and the brain to proper working order.

Green Tourmaline

VENUS ♀, JUPITER ♃

Green Tourmaline occurs in several different color variations, including a warm green tone, similar to a Peridot, and a dark bluish tint.

Like all green gemstones, the Green Tourmaline balances and regulates the physical heart. It calms the nervous system and helps us to relax and regenerate after long illnesses. Its frequency is similar to that of other green things in nature: it connects us with the soothing green of the rain forest and quenches our longing to be enveloped and replenished by Mother Nature.

The balancing Green Tourmaline is in *Nature's Balm* on page A10.

Indigolite and Paraiba

VENUS ♀, MERCURY ☿, JUPITER ♃, NEPTUNE ♆

Indigolite is the blue variety of Tourmaline. It often has some underlying shades of green mixed with the blue. If the stone is more turquoise than blue, it is called Paraiba and is very rare and expensive.

Indigolite and Paraiba belong to the throat chakra, which is the seat of our verbal expression. Both connect the heart with the throat, and thus teach us to speak from the truth in our hearts. Indigolite also calms nervousness and impatience, making this a good stone for students during exams—in the relaxed state induced by Indigolite, we are better able to tap into our memory and knowledge.

Paraiba has a strong Venusian quality. With all the green in the blue, it induces a deep connection to the heart and enables us to express feelings. I think it is a wonderful stone for men to help them to connect with their inner Venus and learn to share from their hearts.

Grace Upon Us on page A8 features Paraiba.

Rubellite

MARS ♂, VENUS ♀, MERCURY ☿, NEPTUNE ♆

The Rubellite, the pink Tourmaline, represents a lover of mankind, one who loves unconditionally and teaches us self-love. Self-love is often difficult to achieve. We know our weaknesses and dark side all too well and are often most unforgiving and hard on ourselves. Beginning in childhood, we learn to reject and negate a large part of our nature, especially our need for love and acceptance within the family. We resign ourselves to making do without those deep needs and we give up vital parts of ourselves. The Rubellite heals and strengthens us, helping us to recover those lost aspects of our nature. With its help, we learn to love ourselves as we are, in all our individuality and beauty. Rubellite helps us to grow and nourish our own needs. As adults, we have the ability to care for ourselves in ways we were not able to do in childhood. We can express our wishes and needs in alignment with our whole being. From that place of self-love and alignment, we want to share and give to the world. The Rubellite opens us up to the abundant love that flows through us in all we do. Our heart is open to joy and exaltation.

Venus and Mars rule the Rubellite in all their different facets. Venus is the goddess of love, harmony, and beauty. She is the muse to artists in all their endeavors. Mars is the pioneer, the warrior who is called to action. Together they help our creativity to be manifested on the earthly plane. They give us the courage and self-esteem to dare to be creative.

Venus and Mars are also eternal lovers. They help us through difficult times in our relationships. They remind us that the bond of love endures beyond all the difficulties that inevitably surface when two personalities merge. It is through our relationship with our intimate partner that we are challenged to grow and examine our behavior and our beliefs. With the solid foundation of love and friendship with our partner, we have the potential to rise out of difficult times, like the Phoenix arising from the ashes.

For a Rubellite example, see *True Heart* on page A12.

Watermelon Tourmaline
MARS ♂, VENUS ♀, MERCURY ☿

The Watermelon Tourmaline is green on the outside and pink on the inside, just as its name implies. It is like Rubellite with a green rind, and thus it has all of the qualities of the Rubellite with the added aspects of patience and compassion. Combing the qualities of love, self-love, patience, and compassion, we are ready to master the affairs of the heart.

Zircon
MERCURY ☿, URANUS ♅

Zircon is a stone with a high light reflection, intense fire, and brilliance. The stones that are most commonly available on the market are white, brown, or blue. Most of the colorless and blue stones are heat treated. I don't object to the heat treatment, because it is a process that is very common in nature. Zircon has a Mohs' hardness of 6½–7 and it is sensitive to knocks and pressure. There are deposits in Cambodia, Burma, Thailand, Sri Lanka, and Vietnam.

Zircon has a relatively high natural radioactivity, making it a strong Uranus representative. If you are very sensitive, you might want to avoid Zircon because of its strength. But Zircon might help someone who is very high strung to relax and to channel those energies better. In any case, you should be cautious in selecting and wearing this stone.

Zircon is the stone for the inventor, the computer wizard, the rebel, and the visionary. It is a stone to support us in our search for what lies beyond concrete, objective reality, a dimension that we know of in our heart and soul. Zircon helps us to step out into new planes of being and to feel comfortable and secure with being different or an outsider.

8

Chakras and Healing Through the Rainbow of Colors

Up to this point, we have learned about the energy and healing properties of gemstones from the point of view of astrology—the relationship between gemstones and their associated planetary principles. In addition to that approach, it is possible to understand the qualities of a gemstone simply by examining its color.

You are already aware of many aspects of your environment that are healing to you: the soothing sound of falling water, the odor of a conifer forest, a bright sunny day. If you look around your home, you will most likely see that consciously or not, you use color in ways that are nurturing and healing for you. Our spirit and our emotions have a powerful response to color. You can tap into this natural response by understanding how color relates to the chakra system and using the color of gemstones to support your current spiritual needs.

To review what you learned in Chapter 2, our evolutionary journey can be represented as the movement of energy through the chakra system. There are seven chakras (energy points), beginning with the base of the spine and leading up to the crown of the head. Energy is moved from one chakra to the next, clearing each chakra as it goes along its path until we reach enlightenment, a state of expanded consciousness where we are at one with the universe. When a chakra is opened up, it becomes a transmitter of divine energy.

The opening of the chakras and the effortless upward rise of the Kundalini can be a delightful process.[1] Each individual experiences this in a very personal way, and yet there are some common features of the process that people describe.

For me, there was a culmination point during a retreat with my Oneness teachers in India, when I felt my head being totally open at the crown—actually physically open, shaped like a bowl with golden petals. My body was bathed in a golden light that permeated every cell. I had a beautiful feeling of expansion and oneness with everything. It was like coming home to myself and being everything. It was love and just *was*.

As you can see, words fail me in trying to describe this experience. The experience of that first moment was very intense. Over the course of the next weeks, I noticed more subtle manifestations of the rising of the Kundalini energy. I still had the sense of being open at the crown and whenever I focused my awareness on that place, the sweetness and golden light would permeate me again. But it felt more subtle and less overpowering than in the beginning. Its impact is still integrating itself into my life today.

It is often the case that the Kundalini does not rise with ease. We can pave the way consciously through spiritual practice, but as we saw in Chapter 2, there are specific challenges and blockages associated with each chakra that must be worked through as we move toward enlightenment. If a chakra is not fully developed or is blocked, it creates specific psychological or physical problems. Thus, there are specific challenges associated with each chakra.

Our physical body is able to use the properties of gemstones and crystals—including their perfect order and alignment, vibrational frequency, and color—to assist this process of moving energy via the chakras. In

....

1 In Eastern teachings, Kundalini is conceptualized as an energy that is coiled up like a serpent at the base of the spine and rises up toward the crown of the head, bringing the freedom of enlightenment and highest consciousness.

this chapter we will learn more about each chakra, the colors associated with it, and the colored gemstones that can support us at each level of the chakra system.

First Chakra: Red and Black

Located in the perineum (the area between the genitals and the anus), the first chakra is called the "root chakra." This chakra is the seat of our physical identity, of our awareness of our existence as a physical body, and the basic survival needs of the body for food, water, shelter, and care. The first chakra connects us to the Earth that supports our existence, making us feel rooted and secure on our home planet and in our bodies.

When we are at the first chakra in our evolution, we are preoccupied with survival issues: making a living, obtaining all that we need for survival, and our fear that we are insufficiently equipped to do that. The first chakra also supplies us with our basic life-force energy. When this chakra is working optimally, we have no survival fears, no doubts of not being in the right place at the right time. We have instead a deep sense of being taken care of and a good supply of life-force energy.

All stones in hues of red and black are helpful for this chakra and its connected issues, including Black Pearl, Bloodstone, Fire Opal, Garnets (Grossular, Almandine, and Pyrope), Rubellite Tourmaline, Ruby, and Spinel. Other first chakra stones include Black Diamond, Black Tourmaline, Black Moonstone, Coral, Hematite, Obsidian, Onyx, and Smoky Quartz.

Second Chakra: Orange

The second chakra, the sacral chakra, is located three fingers below the navel. It is the site of our primary emotions. It is the point of integration of our sexual drive and its accompanying emotions—how we connect with one another emotionally and sexually. The second chakra is the home of the myriad physical and emotional desires that drive us.

As we digest and evaluate our feelings, we try to define who we are in relation to the outside world. The second chakra reflects how truly individuated we are, giving us a sense of self-worth independent from approval of the "tribe"—our friends, family, and society in general.

The orange stones for the second chakra include Amber, Citrine, Fire Opal, Garnet, and Orange-Pink Sapphire. Orange Moonstone and Sunstone are also good second chakra stones.

Third Chakra: Yellow

The third chakra, sometimes called the "power chakra," is located in the solar plexus, midway between the navel and the base of the sternum (the breastbone). Like the first and second chakras, this is also the site of basic animal drives. In the third chakra we expand into our personal power, find our place in the hierarchy of the world, and grow in our creativity and self-expression. Our experience of our self, of our ego, comes into full bloom. If this chakra is blocked, we must face our fears and doubts about our self-worth and deficiencies.

The yellow stones for the third chakra include Beryl, Chrysoberyl Cat's Eye, Citrine, Yellow Diamond, and Yellow Sapphire. Other options are Calcite, Fluorite, Rutilated Quartz, Topaz, and Tiger's Eye.

Fourth Chakra: Pink and Green

The fourth chakra is the heart chakra, located in the center of the chest. In this chakra, we evolve from the animal drives into higher feelings such as love and compassion. Here we learn about self-love, forgiveness, and healing our emotional wounds and lack of trust. We develop a sense of connectedness with beloved ones, our family, our friends, neighbors, other beings, and God. We begin to experience oneness rather than separation.

The heart chakra is the middle chakra between the three upper and lower chakras. This middle location of the heart chakra gives it a special role in balancing us between Heaven and the Earth, the spiritual and physical realms. Pink relates more to the emotional aspects of love and compassion, while green impacts the healing, nourishing, and balancing of the physical heart.

The many stones that support the fourth chakra include Almandine Garnet, Alexandrite, Apatite, Apophyllite Beryl, Chrysoberyl Cat's Eye, Chrysocolla, Chrysoprase, Demantoid Garnet, Dioptase, Emerald, Heliodor (Golden Beryl), Jade, Moonstone, Orange-Pink Sapphire, Peridot, Pearl, Rubellite Tourmaline, Ruby, Spinel, and Watermelon Tourmaline. Even more fourth chakra stones include Malachite, Pink Diamond, Rhodolite, Rhodonite, Rose Quartz, and Topaz.

Fifth Chakra: Blue

In the fifth chakra, located in the throat, we learn to truly express ourselves, to communicate and show ourselves for who we are without hiding or mincing our words. We learn to speak our truth, without fear or expectations, without looking for outside approval. We experience ourselves as individuals, but also as connected with others. At this stage of our evolution we are moving away from the limitations of social rules, beliefs, judgments, and pressures of fitting in with the tribe as we grow into our personal freedom.

In the fifth chakra, blue represents the limitless ocean and sky. The blue stones include Aquamarine, Blue Sapphire, Chrysocolla, Moonstone, Paraiba Tourmaline, Spinel, and Zircon. You may also use Amazonite, Blue Diamond, Blue Opal, Blue Quartz, Blue Topaz, Chalcedony, Fluorite, Iolite, and Turquoise.

Sixth Chakra: Indigo Blue and Violet

The sixth chakra, known as the "third eye," is located slightly above and between the eyebrows. In this chakra we discover our inner direct knowing, intuition, clairvoyance, eternal wisdom, and truth. When this center is developed, we see beyond the physical realm and open our finer inner senses toward a different perception of the inner and outer worlds. Our dual perception of the world is about to be resolved into a higher perspective where we will transcend into a higher state of consciousness. This is a state of oneness with all there is, without separation: the identification with the self begins to dissolve. When there is no self, oneness with God can begin to emerge.

The blue and indigo stones that support this stage of our evolution include Amethyst, Azurite, Blue Sapphire, Indigolite Tourmaline, Labradorite, Lapis Lazuli, Opal, and Tanzanite. Sugilite, Blue Diamond, and Fluorite are also good blue stones.

Seventh Chakra: Gold and White

The seventh chakra, the crown chakra, is located at the top of the head. As the last chakra in the body, this is the place of connection with the eternal consciousness, the divine, the One Spirit, God, the universe—all that is far beyond our limited mind and dual consciousness—until we awaken into self-realization. The Eastern Indian tradition considers enlightenment as a state where there is no self remaining, no ego. God realization is where all that remains is God.

The seventh chakra opens us toward a state of being that is beyond words, a nonconceptual realm. The golden and white stones of the seventh chakra can help us to experience this wordless state. Those stones include Beryl, Diamond, Herkimer Diamond, Quartz, and Zircon. White Sapphire and White Topaz are other seventh chakra stones.

Now you have a basic idea of how the colors of the gemstones relate to your personal voyage of evolution through the chakras. When your attention is drawn to a beautiful pink Rubellite Tourmaline, for example, you can tell simply by its color that this is a stone for the emotional aspects of the heart. Or if you find yourself suddenly attracted to the orange Fire Opals, it might be a sign that you need to pay more attention to your physical body and its energy flow through the first three chakras.

During my own life, as I have grown through a series of thematic life challenges, I have observed corresponding phases of favorite colors in both gemstones and clothing as I seek the colors that support me in each life stage. Since I don't have a very strong Mars in my chart, red and orange have been my favorite colors for most of my life. I wear lots of red clothes; I have red vases filled with poppies, red curtains, a cranberry red bedspread, red pillows, a red recliner, orange lamps, and yellow walls in my home.

During a particular Saturn transit, I was surprised to find myself wearing black—I had not worn black for years. I felt very protected, strengthened, and grounded by black. I also had a green phase that lasted many years—mostly light greens with a yellow undertone like the Peridot. During that period, I was trying to find my heart's desires, heal childhood traumas, and learn to love myself more deeply. And lately pink has invaded my life! I now love to wear pink sweaters for the feelings of love and joy they bring me. I also discovered the Pink Sapphire and Spinel for my own jewelry. Each new color is accompanied by the feelings of sweetness, happiness, and joy that I seek at this stage of my life.

I suggest that you allow yourself to play consciously with colors to discover how each one impacts you. As you reflect on your most and least favorite colors, you may come to further insights into your life challenges and you will be able to choose gemstones to guide and support you in your current life phase.

9

The Metaphysical Aspect of Metals

Are You a Gold or a Silver Person?

In this chapter, we will delve once again into astrological concepts—including the four basic elements of earth, air, fire, and water—to choose one of the most important aspects of a piece of jewelry: the metal that holds the precious stone or crystal. You will discover that all of the elements of a piece of jewelry—stone or crystal, forms and symbols, and metal—reflect complex and rich astrological principles that join us and our jewelry to the macrocosm. You will see that you are not merely subjected to those principles and forces; you can manipulate them to make them work for you as you reach your life goals.

Most women have a strong intuitive preference for either gold or silver jewelry. Like gemstones and crystals, the metals have their own distinctive metaphysical properties that can be used to your advantage. In a nutshell, gold represents the male energy of the Sun, and silver the female energy of the Moon. Your horoscope will reveal which of these heavenly bodies is most important to you, but it will take some thought to decide which of those aspects of yourself you want to strengthen or bring into balance.

Seek Balance by Choosing the
Right Metal for Your Personality

Balance is an important concept in astrology. Just as the universe is a balanced ensemble of opposite forces working in concert, so must we seek balance among the forces in our personality. We can achieve this by expressing the qualities that we have in abundance and supporting those that are lacking. For example, it is not desirable for men to be all masculine, nor for women to be all feminine. Men and women may choose to wear silver or gold, respectively, to balance a predominance of masculine or feminine qualities in their chart or their personality. But some men and women would be better served by wearing the metal that corresponds to their gender if those qualities are weak. And the ideal may be to combine silver and gold in the same piece to balance both energies. Indeed, using both can be cost effective, especially in a large piece, given the rising price of gold.

We are all unique combinations of the four basic cosmic energies: earth, air, fire, and water. The four elements are also classified as masculine (air, fire) or feminine (earth, water) and therefore their importance in your birth chart can be considered when choosing gold or silver jewelry. Later in this chapter you will learn the personality traits associated with each of the four elements.

You may feel that your personality is out of balance, with an excess of some traits and not enough of others. After deciding which aspects of your personality are in need of enhancement, you will be able to choose either gold or silver to strengthen those aspects in order to achieve better balance. Understanding the personality traits associated with each metal will also help you understand why you have an intuitive preference for one or the other.

It may be, though, that you are so pleased with your dominant aspects, such as masculine or feminine, that you choose to enhance that aspect even further by choosing the corresponding rather than the opposite metal. Your intuition is your best guide in all matters of the spirit and jewelry.

Gold: The Sun and Heart Metal

Gold is an element with unique physical and metaphysical properties. Its beauty derives from its golden color and luster. It is the most ductile (meaning that it can be stretched without breaking) and malleable of all metals and can be rolled into exceedingly thin translucent sheets. It is quite resistant to acids and chemicals in general, as well as to moisture and heat, making it well suited to jewelry.

The importance of gold in our lives is truly amazing. It has played a central role in human societies since prehistoric times—in religious objects, coins, jewelry, dentistry, electronics, photography, and even in gourmet food and drinks! Gold has been used for amulets, sacred religious items and statues, and jewelry since ancient time in cultures throughout the world. It has been cherished by the wealthy and powerful to display their status. Historically, gold has played a major economic role—until the Great Depression the gold standard was the basis of our monetary system. Amidst our present-day feelings of economic insecurity and currency instability, the demand for gold is rising, along with its price. As of April 2008, gold is valued around $930 per ounce. Experts are forecasting that it will rise to as high as $1,800 an ounce.

Gold also has important medical applications. Colloidal gold (minute particles of gold suspended in water) is used by some alternative medicine practitioners for conditions of the heart, depression, rheumatoid arthritis, and glandular and neurological conditions. We will see in a moment how some of those uses of gold are explained by astrology.

Isn't it fascinating to note how many aspects of our lives are impacted by gold? Around the world and throughout the ages, gold has been and continues to be the most cherished metal for jewelry. Today, even with the rising price of gold, most of us are able to own gold jewelry. Like the kings and queens of history, we are able today to celebrate our abundance and self-love by wearing gold jewelry.

Life Comes from the Sun

The Sun sustains our entire planet and each of us as individuals with its life-giving energy. All life on this planet turns toward the energy of the Sun. Hence, the Sun is accorded a central role in astrology.

We all worship the Sun! Most people are affected physically and emotionally by a long period of cloudy skies, and we reawaken each spring as the days lengthen and the weather warms so we can be outside in the Sun. We seek the life-giving rays of the Sun on beaches everywhere. I recall being in Anchorage, Alaska, one July. The temperature was 50 degrees—freezing by my Hawaiian standards—and I was amazed to see everyone outside in T-shirts and shorts, exposing themselves to the Sun after the long, dark Alaskan winter. I think of sunbathing as a Sun meditation: being still and connected with our own self, nature, and God.

Following the traditions of all human cultures on the Earth in creating beautiful, lasting jewelry from gold, we align ourselves with the life-giving, healing energy of the Sun.

Our Sun Center: The Heart

Life is consciousness itself! In astrology, the Sun represents the center of our being, our self-awareness, identity, and life force, as well as our highest state of consciousness. It is our true nature. In jewelry, gold is beneficial when you feel you have lost your center or your identity, bringing you into alignment with the Sun.

If the Sun has hard aspects with the outer planets in your birth chart, you will need to make sure to balance and support your Sun. Without that balance and support there will be constant friction around expressing yourself in a healthy way and you might have challenges with health problems, especially with your heart.

The Sun, as the center of our solar system, corresponds to the heart, which is approximately in the center of the body. The heart is said to be the seat of our emotions and feelings of love and compassion. As we saw in Chapter 2, the heart is the middle chakra that divides the upper chakras from the lower. In the first three chakras, we are occupied with our physical survival and developing an ego and self-identification.

When we reach the heart, we have the opportunity to truly go beyond our own needs and wants and to experience love, connectedness, and compassion for others. After that experience we can move on into the higher chakras and experience an increasing state of connectedness and oneness with God and our true nature.

So you can see the importance of the Sun, the heart, and hence of gold for your spiritual growth. In homeopathy gold is administered for conditions of the heart—not only medical but psychological, including depression and suicidal thoughts—which is consistent with the meaning of the Sun in astrology. When our psyche is weak, when we are stymied in bringing forth expression of our true selves in the way we are living, we lose our center and become depressed. *Then we need gold!*

Because of its association with the heart, gold is the perfect metal for a wedding band, the symbol of pure and eternal love and commitment between two people.

Choosing the Right Type of Gold

There are many ways to take advantage of the healing aspects of gold. My preferred application is obviously to wear it on my body in the form of beautiful jewelry. This way we work with its electromagnetic frequency and let it radiate into our energetic system.

In making jewelry, gold is combined with other metals, such as silver and copper, to form an alloy. The percentage, or purity, of gold in the alloy is expressed in karats. Pure gold is 24 karats. An alloy with 75 percent gold is 18 karats; 58.5 percent gold is 14 karats.

"White gold," actually silvery in color, is an alloy with whitish metals such as palladium, platinum, or nickel. I use only palladium in my white gold pieces. Nickel has been shown to be a very problematic metal for jewelry. Since many people (12–15 percent of women) have allergic skin reactions to it. Europe, Japan, and China have banned or limited the use of nickel in jewelry. In the United States, jewelry that contains nickel must be so labeled.

I find that wearing white gold does not have the same effect as yellow gold. I feel that removing the natural yellow color of gold detracts from its true representation as the Sun metal.

In order to maximize the metaphysical qualities of gold jewelry and benefit from the strongest frequencies, you should select the purest gold that you can afford, preferably 18, 22, or 24 karats, which is what I use in my own designs. There is nothing more satisfying than the feel of a heavy 24-karat gold band around your finger. However, 24-karat gold is very soft and will bend and get nicked quite easily; such a gold ring has to be heavy enough in the shank (the part that goes around the underside of the finger) to make it durable.

Silver: The Moon Metal

Silver, though less precious than gold (the current price in 2008 is about $18 an ounce), also has special physical characteristics that make it highly valued in many applications. It is very ductile and malleable and can be highly polished. It conducts electricity and heat extremely well. Its very high reflectivity makes it of value for making mirrors and in photography. Silver is used in coins, utensils, electronics, dentistry, batteries, and more. Colloidal silver is used by alternative medical practitioners for its antibacterial properties.

A drawback of silver is that it tarnishes with exposure to air. A great deal of jewelry is made of silver because it is so much cheaper than gold. Some people also prefer the white color of silver.

We learned earlier that the Moon enfolds the feminine principles of receptivity, nurturing, motherhood, giving life, giving and receiving, our unconscious mind, fantasy, creativity, safety, and feelings. Like a mirror, the Moon reflects the light of the Sun, lighting our way in the dark of night.

I have observed that many women who prefer silver for their jewelry have a strong Cancer or Moon position in their astrological chart, or a lot of water energy. For them, it is intuitively natural to flow with the Moon energy represented by silver. Often girls wear silver jewelry but change to gold as they grow up. This is partly because they are better able to afford silver when they are young, but also because young people need the support of silver while they are reflecting on their life experience and learning from it. Later on when we have reached a point in our personal evolution where we feel more centered in our ego, having reached a place of some maturity in our male Sun (such as with self-expression), we often change to gold.

Often it is helpful for men to wear silver to support their inner connection with their feminine side, intuition, creativity, imagination—their inner woman. But if a man has a lot of water energy in his chart or a strong Cancer or Moon position, gold is essential to achieve balance.

For women it is generally more helpful to wear gold to support decisiveness and self-expression and to help integrate the inner male aspects. If a woman has a lot of fire energy in her chart and problems around finding and expressing her feminine side, silver should be considered.

Sometimes I recommend using both metals in one piece of jewelry to help to balance male and female energy aspects—your intuition will guide you in choosing the right metal for your gender aspects.

The Four Elements and Their Connection to Gold and Silver

You can use the elemental associations of the planets in your chart to determine your preferred metal. Since each element has a distinct profile, your unique combination may reveal much about you.

Earth

Earth is considered a feminine energy in astrology and is thus represented by silver. Earth is a concentrated form of matter and, contrary to air and fire, is subject to the force of gravity, which makes people who have a dominant earth aspect in the astrological chart prone to slow yet deliberate and thorough action. They may be slow to change, but the end result is usually positive. Earth people manifest self-discipline, patience, organization, structure, intelligence, logic, stubbornness, strength, fanaticism, and sensual joy. They apply their keen minds in a realistic, down-to-earth way. They are likely to study a goal and go about achieving it methodically.

Earth people are skilled in using and manipulating reality and the material world to gain access to worldly pleasures and riches, satisfying the earthly desires. They are creators. They dominate, structure, and rule the material world. They can be artists, sculptors, gardeners, accountants, car mechanics, doctors, or politicians.

Water

Water is the most feminine energy in astrology, represented by silver. Water is very adaptable: it conforms to the shape of its container and willingly flows downhill. Water people are very receptive and responsive. They experience the world first through their perceptions and emotional filter. They are easily impacted by what others say to them or simply by being in the energy field of another person. Usually they go through constant emotional changes because of their fluidity and their empathetic nature. They have a tendency to dream, to be melancholic, to prefer quiet comfort, and to be very intuitive and artistically creative. Water people do well in the supporting, healing, and nurturing roles, where their empathetic nature is needed: nurses, counselors, psychologists, doctors, mothers, secretaries, or working with children.

Air

Air is a male energy, associated with gold. Air is the most flexible and fluid state because of its gaseous consistency. Air exists between things, encompasses and surrounds everything on the Earth. In that sense, air is a mediator, a connector, a communicator. Air people are extremely adaptable to new situations. Air represents the mind, and air people approach the world first and foremost through their minds (rather than emotions), quickly sizing up and responding to situations and challenges. Air people, such as myself, love astrology for its potential for understanding the world. We use astrology and our mental bent to reflect on our feelings. Their openness to higher wisdom and knowledge

makes air people excellent inventors, innovative thinkers, and teachers—the rebels and founders of philosophical movements in the world.

Fire

Fire is the most male energy in astrology, represented by gold. It manifests as an abundance of physical energy and the need to move and experience life in all its facets. Fire people display a long list of powerful
qualities: gregariousness, strength, power, vigor, adventurousness, ambi-
tion, single-mindedness of purpose, courage, impatience, self-trust, ide-
alism, passion, ruthlessness, self-centeredness, strong emotions, a warrior
stance, dominance, anger, initial spark, warmth, and impulsivity.

Fire people have strong leadership qualities. Often they are very
charismatic and driven by their passions and goals in life. To be truly
happy and fulfilled, fire people need to find a profession in which they
can lead rather than follow. They often choose to create their own enterprise or take on top administrative positions in major corporations.
They are not good followers—when told what to do, they become an-
gry and bitter. They like to carry responsibility and because they have
so much energy they are hard workers and overachievers. The male aspect of fire likes to take initiative, shake and move the world, and leave
a lasting impact.

How to Evaluate the Elements in Your Chart

Each sign of the zodiac is assigned to one of the elements. For example, the fire signs are Aries, Leo, and Sagittarius. The planets are further
assigned a point value to indicate their relative importance. The Sun,
which we have seen is the most important heavenly body, and the ascendant are assigned the maximum of 10 points. The outer planets have
less influence and receive only four points each. Here is the complete

list of the point values of the planets plus the Ascendant[1] and the Mid-heaven[2]:

RELATIVE IMPORTANCE OF THE PLANETS, ASCENDANT, & MIDHEAVEN

Planet; Point on Horizon	Point Value (Out of 10)
Ascendant	10
Midheaven	7
Sun	10
Moon	8
Venus	5
Mars	5
Mercury	5
Jupiter	5
Saturn	5
Pluto	4
Uranus	4
Neptune	4
Chiron	4

Your astrological chart indicates how many planets you have in each of the four elements according to the zodiac sign the planet falls into. By adding up the points in each element, you will be able to determine to what extent each element influences your personality. There is a total of 76 points. If you have more than half of the total in one element, this element will dominate how you express yourself in the world.

....

1 The point on the zodiac that is rising over the eastern horizon at the moment and place of your birth. The Ascendant has great importance because it casts its influence over everything else in your chart. Therefore, it receives as many points as the Sun.

2 The Midheaven is the point highest above the horizon as shown by the cusp of the Tenth House (the line between the Ninth and Tenth Houses). It symbolizes your destiny in this life. It is considered an important indicator of your most important life goals, including career.

In reality, we all have some aspects of each of the four elements, but still you will find dominant tendencies in your chart. By understanding those tendencies, you will be empowered to make better life choices and to discover how to balance and support your personality.

If you don't have any points at all in one element, it either doesn't play a big role in your life, you might have brought it with you as potential from a past life, or you experience it as a challenge. For example, if you don't have any earth in your chart, it might be that you are challenged in the areas of organizing your life, following through with things, maintaining order and discipline, and acquiring and budgeting money. The absence of an element in your chart may be either significant or inconsequential—it is up to you to reflect on the course of your life and determine what is missing or overabundant.

In Chapter 6 we looked at Anne's chart on page 75. The planets on her chart are distributed among the elements like this:

DISTRIBUTION OF PLANETS AMONG
THE ELEMENTS ON ANNE'S CHART

Element	Planets in That Element on Anne's Chart	Total Points for Planets
Fire	Saturn, Uranus, Pluto	13
Air	Moon, Venus, Ascendant, Chiron	29
Earth	Sun, Mercury, Jupiter, Midheaven	25
Water	Mars, Neptune	9

From the above, we have a general idea about how Anne expresses herself energetically in her life. Her strongest available energies, waiting to be used and expressed, are earth and air. Those elements make her very realistic, intelligent, grounded, systematic in her work, organized, determined, and patient and enduring when needed. She has a good connection with the physical world. The slow and cautious energy of earth will be offset to some extent in Anne by the influence of air, which makes her fast, flexible, spontaneous, intellectually oriented due to her strong mind, and curious. Anne is always seeking understanding and searching for new horizons. Air brings qualities of impatience and speed to all that she undertakes. The combination of earth and air makes Anne a good candidate for professions that combine intellect, organization, and concrete creativity, such as a sculptor or architect.

Fire is available but not in the foreground in Anne's chart. Physical energy is available if needed but is not abundant. Therefore, self-expression and leadership are not overly strong.

Water is the weakest of the elements in Anne's chart. Water represents feelings and the unconscious, a tendency toward melancholy, and the ability to be strongly impacted by other people's feelings. The weakest element points to a challenge that needs to be examined. Anne will probably use her mind and determination to inquire into the depths of the human mind and spirit in order to offset her weak water element and make a deeper contact with her own unconscious emotions.

The Four Elements and the Metals

Now that you understand the importance and meaning of the four elements, you can choose the right metal to support your specific configuration of the elements in your astrological chart. You realize now that choosing gold or silver is not merely a matter of appearance!

We have seen that gold represents the Sun, which immediately relates it to fire and male energy. Silver represents the Moon, which is a water planet, and feminine energy. If, for example, you already have plenty of fire energy in your makeup, it might not be the best choice for you to wear gold—perhaps adding fire to fire would be too hot for you! You may choose instead to favor the receptive and feminine qualities of silver, especially if you are a man.

If a man has a lot of water (a feminine element) in his chart, he is bound to encounter some challenges around finding his own maleness and coming to terms with what it means for him to be a man. In this case, gold would come to his aid by strengthening the masculine fire aspect.

At times people prefer to wear the metal corresponding to their dominant element. I have met many Cancer (water) women with a great deal of water in their chart who would only wear silver jewelry. Their dominant feminine water ways are what come most naturally to them and they don't wish for more fire in their interactions.

Sometimes the homeopathic approach of using a high potency of a poison, which would create exactly the symptoms we want to relieve, is the way to go. I can give no exact recipe for all people: we are all individuals and have unique needs for our journey. I don't want to tell you exactly what to put in your suitcase! I recommend that you always follow your intuition and preferences, because your inner voice is ultimately connected to your deepest needs and desires.

If after studying your chart, you are in doubt as to whether to favor your masculine or feminine qualities, or which of the four elements you would like to enhance, you can always use both gold and silver in the same piece of jewelry to achieve balance and harmony.

In the next chapter, we will bring together all that you have learned about your spiritual needs, gemstones, and metals to find just the right piece of jewelry. It is time for you to follow in the footsteps of royalty and enter into the kingdom of precious jewels to delight your eye and nurture your soul!

10

Designing the Perfect
Piece of Jewelry

Until reading this book, you may have been aware of jewelry only as objects of beauty and adornment. Now you know that gemstones are tiny representatives of the cosmos that incorporate the same astrological principles that orchestrate the dance of the planets across the heavens, and that gemstones can bring healing and supporting energy into your life. You learned in the last chapter that the metals, gold and silver, manifest those same principles. In fact, every aspect of a piece of jewelry plays a role in the metaphysical impact of the piece, and a good jeweler carefully considers each aspect when designing a unique piece for the specific needs of an individual.

In this chapter, you will learn about the final design elements that determine a piece of jewelry's metaphysical meaning and power: symbols and shapes.

Conscious Design in the Process of Creating Jewelry

"Conscious design" refers to the very deliberate selection of each aspect of a jewelry piece to achieve a specific result. It is an empowering, essential process for creating Jewelry for the Soul. We can use conscious design to balance and bring harmony through beauty into our lives.

There is, however, an important intuitive component to conscious design. I am usually very intuitive in my process of creation.

With the *Precious Jewels* ring on page A11, for example, I have intuitively mixed different shapes such as several circular stones and a pear-shaped one. The result is a very harmonious, balanced ensemble that emphasizes the nourishing qualities of the gems.

Sometimes I perceive a design when I hold a stone in my hand. Sometimes it evolves in the process of work at the bench or in creating the design with the client. In any case, creating a piece of jewelry involves carefully assembling exactly the right elements for the right effect.

This process has been known since ancient times, when people created amulets and talismans—empowered magical objects, often with runes (magical written characters). I don't discount the power of symbols such as runes, but I do not use organized magical practices or invocations in my own life or in my jewelry. I prefer to seek understanding and growth through a personalized spiritual path. I use the inherent metaphysical properties of gemstones and metals and the most basic forms and symbols of the spiral, circle, triangle, and square.

The first consideration in conscious design is, of course, beauty. Beauty is the most basic language of our soul and connects us to the natural world. In general, you can assume that something you find beautiful is harmonizing and supportive of your needs. And now let us go beyond beauty to the specific power of forms and symbols.

The Language of Symbols

Symbols are the intuitive language of the soul. Our dreams are full of symbols that express our deepest unconscious fears and desires. We all dream in symbols without ever consciously learning how to use symbols in our dreams, reflecting that we all belong to a "collective unconscious" that ties the human community together. "Archetypes"—the instinctual symbols that represent human experience, such as the mother and the father—exist in all people across all cultures.

Symbols have a very important place in jewelry design. Using symbols in jewelry allows us to open ourselves to a higher consciousness and to bring higher forces into active presence in our lives.

Each symbol, like each gemstone, has a unique energetic signature. We saw earlier that you can use kinesiology to test the impact of different substances on yourself, including gemstones. You can also use it to verify how the energy of different symbols affects you in order to choose those that have the most benefit for you.

Sacred Geometry

In the very center of Cologne, Germany, where I grew up, there is a magnificent cathedral called the Cologne Cathedral, or the *Kölner Dom*. Construction on the cathedral began in 1248 and took six hundred years to complete! As you exit the central railroad station, you find yourself directly in front of this imposing structure and are awestruck by its size and beauty. When I felt upset about something as a young person, I would go to the Dom and just sit in the pews. The moment I entered the Dom I would be infused with the stillness and sacredness of the church. The peacefulness of that place would quiet my inner uproar of thoughts and feelings. I felt the powerful energy of the building and loved the beauty of this church (and others) and the medieval art that lined the walls. In those days, churches were always open to people who needed comforting sanctuary.

Churches and temples used to be built according to the metaphysical laws of "sacred geometry," derived from the mathematical order of the universe. I believe that this is what creates the *inner* peace and silence that we feel there.

You need only look skyward at night to the patterns of the stars to realize that certain shapes occur throughout the cosmos and relate to the origin of the universe and everything in it.

It was believed in medieval and ancient times that the entire natural world is constructed from a sort of blueprint of the same geometric patterns, and that these basic forms have spiritual meaning and power. The mathematical ratios of those forms were studied carefully because it was believed that they revealed the physical and metaphysical laws of the universe. Numbers therefore were also considered to be metaphysical symbols. Those mathematical principles were incorporated into the design of churches, religious art, music, and so on. While some may be skeptical of this idea, it is hard not to feel the awesome power and beauty of the great cathedrals designed according to sacred geometry.

Perhaps because of my early experience at the cathedral of Cologne, spiritual geometry has impacted my jewelry designs. In sacred geometry, the basic shapes take on symbolic meaning. Those shapes are found all over the world in churches and temples, at holy sites, and etched into cave walls throughout human history.

The four basic shapes used in jewelry design are the spiral, circle, triangle, and square. All four are found throughout creation and have spiritual significance.

The Spiral of Life

We saw in Chapter 3 that the spiral is an archetypal building block of the universe, appearing everywhere in nature. It is a powerful symbol of life, growth, and evolution. As the most dynamic symbol, illustrating the unending cycle of change, it is a major element in my jewelry designs, especially in pendants, rings, and earrings. I love the dynamic energy and beauty of spirals. My trademark spiral clasp is a way to use the clasp of a necklace as a centerpiece and pendant.

By wearing a spiral design in your jewelry you can open your soul and your life to more fluidity, energy, and the grace of guidance from a higher intelligence and the divine.

See *Milky Way* on page A10 for a spiral piece of jewelry.

The Circle

The circle is the ancient symbol for God, the endless, all-encompassing oneness of consciousness on all levels of creation. Representing fundamental unity with God and all creation.

The circle and its three-dimensional form, the sphere, are the most balanced and harmonizing of all forms, and for that reason they are widely used in religious and secular art, for example in Hindu mandalas—geometric designs that represent the universe and the cosmos. Mandalas are based on the circle, in which different patterns emerge out of the center, as in the Tibetan tanka paintings.

The circle is also the astrological symbol for the Sun.

A ring is of course a closed circle. A wedding band symbolizes the unbroken, eternal oneness, and commitment of a couple. The wedding band encircles the Venus finger,[1] which connects directly to the heart, symbolizing encircling the heart as a pledge of eternal love and fidelity.

If you, like I, have a great deal of tension and friction in your horoscope, jewelry designed around the circle may bring harmony and balance into your life.

I use circles extensively in my jewelry. I love the balance and harmony of the circle. Round stones and circular forms in my jewelry help smooth out the tension and friction in my own life. See one of my circle pieces, *Divine Intervention*, on page A7.

The Triangle

The triangle is based on the number three, the trinity of life. There are two kinds of triangles: upright and inverted. The upright triangle represents masculine principles, fire, prosperity, and spirit. The inverted triangle represents the feminine principles of mother, earth, water, and grace. The hexagram, also called the six-rayed star or Star of David, combines both triangles and therefore balances feminine and masculine; it symbolizes balance and knowledge. Some people like to wear the six-rayed star to enhance their connection with spirit or the spiritual realm.

In astrology, a triangle called a trigon is formed when three planets are at an angle of 120 degrees to each other. A trigon signifies a harmonic energy flow between the planets, which makes it easy to find a way to express the connected principles.

I sometimes use triangular stones for rings in my jewelry. The triangle makes an interesting form with an easy dynamic flow. For an example of a triangular ring, see *Show me my Destiny* on page A11.

....

1 In palmistry, each finger is associated with a particular planet and reflects personality traits.

The Square

The square represents the Earth and the material realm. It symbolizes stability, firmness, balance, and the number four. In astrology, it signifies a difficult and tense aspect (an angle of 90 degrees) between two planets in a natal chart. Planetary principles that are connected with a square call attention to themselves strongly and force us to learn and grow in the area they represent.

Leonardo da Vinci's drawing "Vitruvian Man" shows a man set into both a circle and a square in order to illustrate the perfect proportions of the human body. Leonardo believed that the human body was analogous to the workings of the macrocosm. His drawing unites the two realms of human existence: material (square) and spiritual (circle).

I don't make much jewelry based on the square, because I find my connection with the material world in the metals and stones I work with. That seems sufficient for me, but you may be drawn to the square for its aesthetic or spiritual properties.

Most of us are in need of greater equilibrium in our life as we try to balance the opposing forces in our personality and all of the demands that are made upon our body, mind, and spirit. For this reason, we are intuitively drawn to balanced, symmetrical, and harmonious forms, which create a sense of alignment. You feel this immediately when you enter a cathedral or other carefully designed building that uses form to enhance the inner calm that we all seek. The same principles that were used to create the Cologne Cathedral can be applied to your next piece of jewelry!

Necklace, Ring, Pendant, or Earrings?

Your next consideration will be the type of jewelry. The choice of necklace, ring, pendant, or earrings may depend on the chakra that is in need of support, corresponding to organs of the body such as the heart or mind. For example, the Ruby is a wonderful stone to wear in a pendant over the heart, as are all the beautiful green specimens.

The same gemstone may have a different impact according to where it is worn on the body. For example, you might choose to wear Herkimer Diamonds as earrings to balance the right and left sides of your brain. When worn over the heart, the Herkimer Diamond strengthens the aura and shields against electromagnetic radiation. If worn over the thymus (just behind the sternum), it activates the immune system. The Herkimer Diamond will do all of this to some extent when worn in the energy field, but it will work more potently when put in the right place.

I love to make and wear rings. A ring offers much pleasure because you can look at it frequently, turn it around, and enjoy how it sparkles in the changing light. Earrings offer more pleasure to others who see you wearing them.

Finally, you will choose the forms that correspond to the principles you seek to incorporate into your spiritual journey.

11

Finding and Empowering the Perfect Piece of Jewelry for Your Heart and Soul

You now have a good understanding of the astrological principles that are at work in your life and the main areas of challenge that you want to address. You know how gemstones manifest those principles. You have identified several gemstones that can support your areas of challenge and the principles that you want to focus on. You have chosen either gold or silver, or both, according to their role in your spiritual unfolding. And finally, you have identified the shapes that correlate with where you are in that process.

Now you're ready to put all of those elements together into the perfect piece of jewelry. After getting a general idea of the piece you want, you will find a jeweler, have the piece made, and do a cleansing and empowering ritual to prepare the piece to do its best work in supporting your goals and needs.

Be Guided by Your Inner Wisdom—
In Life and In Your Jewelry

You now have some technical expertise with astrology, gemstones, metals, and shapes. But your inner wisdom and intuitive sense of beauty are just as important in finding or creating the perfect piece of jewelry. In fact, my goal is to empower you to trust your own feelings and sense of beauty in all areas of your life. Your jewelry will be an important manifestation of your spiritual knowledge, your goals for your life journey, and your personal aesthetic sense. Be thoughtful, but also trust your inner wisdom. If a piece of jewelry strongly appeals to your intuition and sense of beauty, it will undoubtedly also have the spiritual properties you seek.

Your perfect piece of jewelry will be a reminder to yourself and a message to the world about who you are: your spiritual values, your self-love and acceptance, and your intention to become your best self. Gemstones and crystals are channels that allow grace to flow into your life. In carefully selecting your jewelry, you are consciously choosing to support weak areas and inviting grace to turn those vices into virtues. You will learn in this chapter how to invest your jewelry with your thoughts and feelings so that it is empowered to help you manifest them.

Stone Considerations

There's more to choosing a stone than just the type! While you'll ultimately choose the particular stone that speaks to you, there are a few more considerations to narrow your search.

Natural or Synthetic Stones?

What is real and true is always empowering and uplifting. Gemstones and crystals have been created throughout the evolution of our Mother Earth in a furnace of unimaginable heat and pressure. No laboratory can duplicate those conditions. I invite you to trust in the alchemy of that natural process of creation in the womb of the Mother.

I can enjoy the beauty of a synthetic stone, which might have the same appearance, chemical composition, and hardness as the natural stone. But I am very aware that it will not have the highest empowering impact for my spirit.

Sometimes I do use Diamonds and Sapphires that have been heat treated to improve the color. I feel that heat treatment does not diminish the beneficial radiance of these stones; it merely enhances their beauty. But for my personal jewelry and the jewelry I create, I stay away from man-made stones.

What Makes a Good Stone?

There are both objective and subjective qualities that make a good stone. Jewelers choose stones for their color, translucency, clarity, perfection of the cut, and reflectivity. Those qualities are all related to the price of the stone. But you will also choose the best stone for you by the beauty you perceive, your intuitive response to it, and how it impacts your energy.

The Indian Vedic astrology and Ayurvedic traditions, which both use gemstones for healing purposes, suggest using large stones of at least 2 carats. The cost of such a stone might often be prohibitive—a 2-carat Ruby could cost more than $3,000!—and you might not want to have such a large stone for your jewelry. In my experience, even a small stone can have a decisive impact on the body's energy field. As mentioned previously, you can directly observe the power of even small stones with kinesiology.

I feel that your alignment with the energy pattern of a specific stone is more important than the size of the stone. That alignment is perceived through your sense of beauty or through testing. That is the reason why you might find a piece of Soul Jewelry already made and waiting for you somewhere in a store. It might be just perfect as it is!

Mass Produced or Handcrafted?

With globalization we are increasingly living in a world in which goods and services are provided by people who work in very harsh conditions and are paid next to nothing for their labor. These practices are not in harmony with spiritual principles, which call for honoring and enhancing the worth and dignity of each human being. One way of putting your spiritual values into practice is to avoid buying these mass-produced products. You can choose instead to support craftspeople and artists who do their own work and businesses that pay a living wage and provide humane working conditions.

Jewelers, as opposed to jewelry factories, invest a great deal of themselves in the conception and creation of beautiful jewelry. This is an intensely personal art and much is lost when jewelry is mass produced in a negative factory setting. I give lovingly of myself as I strive to create my best possible work for my clients, knowing how important each piece may be to someone.

Jewelry making is a passion that we pursue in spite of the hardships of the profession—the large investment in tools, setting up a workshop, and expensive materials (gold, silver, platinum, and gemstones)—with no guarantee of a return on our investment. Sometimes when I see cheap mass-produced jewelry in a store I feel very frustrated because there is no way I can compete with it in terms of price. On the other hand, mass-produced pieces can never compete with jewelry hand-crafted by an artist. You will never feel the satisfaction and joy that a work of art, a beautiful, lovingly handcrafted one-of-a-kind piece will give you. Honoring and enjoying such a piece of jewelry is a way of celebrating your own individuality and value.

Jewelry is a luxury by nature and therefore expensive. This is as it should be. Jewelry is created from the most beautiful and precious metals and gemstones our planet has to offer, and it is shaped through human touch and creativity into something that might last for generations. Passed on as an heirloom, it will tell a story to your children's children about your desires, values, sense of beauty, and abilities. It could even end up in a museum at some point! Jewelry for the Soul is even more than that: it is an expression of your most important spiritual values and goals, self-love, generosity, or love for others.

Jewelry has this transcending, timeless quality because of its materials, which are almost eternal. When you look at Roman and Egyptian jewelry in museums, you see that the simple designs of jewelry are also timeless. Timeless beauty speaks to our human senses and soul.

I encourage you to wait to purchase your Jewelry for the Soul until you are able to afford a piece that you really like. It is better to save up for the perfect piece than to buy lesser pieces that don't really speak to your soul. On the other hand, if you fall in love with a specific stone, it is best to buy it immediately because you will never encounter the same stone again. You can wait to have it made into jewelry until you can afford it.

You now have all the information you need to seek out a jeweler and start working on your perfect piece!

You and Your Jeweler

If you are looking for a special piece of jewelry, you can either purchase it ready made or work with a jeweler to create exactly the right piece. You may spy a piece in a shop window and fall in love with it on sight. You will be drawn to the gemstone, the metal, and the design and will know intuitively, from the beauty and feel of the piece, "*This is what I need.*"

If you are looking for something designed more specifically for your soul's needs and potential and want to be more aware of how each element of a piece of jewelry contributes to its spiritual character, you may want to find a spiritually oriented jeweler who has the skill and knowledge to help you put together the perfect piece. You should feel drawn to both the jeweler's work and personality.

I work closely with my clients to design a piece of jewelry that fits their unique spiritual needs and their personal sense of beauty. If you choose this path, you will find that you have a deeper connection with the piece. I find this collaborative process exhilarating as I get to know my clients' deepest spiritual needs and life goals. It is very satisfying for me to know that I play a role in their well-being. You will find that when you take an active part in this process you will take away with you a piece of jewelry to wear all your life and possibly a better understanding of where you want to go in life and how to get there.

If you work with a jeweler, you will begin by identifying the spiritual principles that you want to focus on in your life, perhaps by means of an astrological reading. Then you will choose the gemstones, the metal, and the shapes that will support those principles. You will want to hold several different gemstones in your hand to find the one that feels just right—remember that no two stones are alike.

Reading the Personal Aura

Much of my process of creating Jewelry for the Soul comes by way of my intuition and psychic abilities, which I have sought to fine tune over the years. As I consider all the elements that go into a piece of jewelry, I try to get a deep sense of my client: of the individual's personality, needs, concerns, and goals. One aspect of the client that is particularly helpful to me is the auric field around the body.

The aura is a field of energy that radiates out from the body in colored layers. In Japan it is called "Ki," in China "Chi," and Austrian-American psychoanalyst Wilhelm Reich called it "Orgon." The existence of an electromagnetic field around objects is now accepted by scientists, who refer to it as the "bio field."

I believe that some people—clairvoyants—are able to see the auric field. Although I am not clairvoyant, I am able to tune into the aura to some extent. From the strength and color of the aura, it is possible to learn about a person's physical and emotional health. When I give an astrological reading prior to creating a piece of jewelry, I get a deeper sense of the person by studying all the exterior clues the person presents, including manner of speech, clothing, body language, and the aura. All of that information goes into a piece of Jewelry for the Soul.

Create a Cleansing and Empowering Ritual

In view of all the time, thought, and money that you have invested in finding this perfect piece, I encourage you to enhance its potential to do its intended work in your life by preparing it with a cleansing and empowering ritual.

Gemstones have already had a very long life before they come to you to be worn on your body. They have gone through incredible stresses in their creation and have been handled by many people, often working under conditions of extreme hardship, beginning with mining. Some gemstones are involved in violence and subject to greed. Since you know that gemstones have an energy field that interacts with the energy fields of other beings, it is not difficult to imagine that a gemstone could have acquired some negative energy in its long history. You don't want to carry this negative baggage with you! A ritual can cleanse the stone of this negative energy, freeing up its power to positively impact your own energy field.

Spiritual rituals have been performed by all cultures for thousands of years. Even today, in the scientific age, we continue to believe in the power of these rituals, and in the power of prayer, to influence our lives in some way. We use rituals to connect with the divine, so that the divine may hear our wishes and act with us to manifest them.

During a recent trip to India, I witnessed a great many religious rituals. While I didn't necessarily identify with the complex system of deities of Hinduism, I must admit that I experienced palpable sensations of well-being during these rituals. It was clear to me that something powerful was taking place, perhaps related to the combined impact of millions of people practicing these ceremonies over thousands of years.

I think of rituals and prayer as a sort of telephone line, an open channel to the divine that allows grace to flow through us. This is what you want to achieve with a cleansing and empowering ritual for your new jewelry.

Your ritual will be designed around your specific spiritual needs, what you want this particular piece of jewelry to do for you. We begin with a consideration of the four basic elements and how their influence can be used to enhance the power of your jewelry. You may review Chapter 9 to remind yourself of the basic qualities of earth, water, air, and fire.

Earth is abundantly alive, creating, nurturing, and healing all forms of life in its realm. For cleansing, you could use those unique qualities by sprinkling soil or beach sand on your piece of jewelry. Some people bury their crystals in a hole in the ground for a while—just don't forget where the hole is! It is most powerful to do this around the time of the full moon, because the Earth's power rises to the surface at this time.[1]

Water is an obvious choice for a cleansing ritual—but how are you to find water that is actually clean and maximally energized? It helps if you have a river, lake, or the ocean nearby, but even those may be spoiled by toxins, bacteria, and harmful residues from factories and farms.

I'm afraid that your tap water doesn't qualify for cleansing. It is not enough that the water be reasonably free of bacteria and toxins—it must also be energized. Dr. Masaru Emoto's photographs of crystallized water from a variety of sources (oceans, lakes, tap water, holy water, and so on) show the impact of toxicity and exposure to different thoughts of feelings. Thoughts of love, appreciation, and gratitude form the most beautiful and balanced crystals. Water exposed to thoughts of hate or anger shows ugly, unformed crystals.

So please begin by using the purest water you can find. Bless the water and say a prayer expressing your wish to use the cleansing and energizing qualities of the water. Then lay your piece of jewelry in the water briefly.

Salt water is sometimes recommended for cleansing and energizing healing gemstones and crystals. I disagree with this. Salt water is corrosive and can actually destroy some gemstones and crystals—the fragile Opals, for example. I recommend that you avoid salt water.

Air is often incorporated into rituals by burning incense. Incense contains stimulants that work directly on our limbic brain (the seat of our emotions), bypassing the conscious mind. Certain smells can awaken long-buried memories and the feelings associated with them.

Incense and etheric oils (healing oils such as rosemary, lavender, peppermint, and wintergreen) are used in rituals to install a sacred and contained atmosphere. The incense cleanses the spaces in preparation for the ceremony.

....

1 The influence of the full moon on the Earth is well known to science and used by farmers to their advantage when they plant and harvest according to the phases of the Moon. Healing herbs are picked at the full moon, when they are at full strength.

Fire is wild, destructive, and often untamable—and yet it is also cleansing and brings new life. When a fire destroys an entire forest, the burned trees fertilize the soil and new life grows from the blackened ground. Many cultures burn their dead and let the lifeless body be transformed and given back to the Earth, giving rise to new life. Learning to tame fire marked an important evolutionary step for our ancestors, as they could cook food to destroy pathogens, warm themselves even in the Arctic cold, and keep threatening animals at bay.

Fire has always been considered sacred and played a role in religious rites of all kinds. It symbolizes the Sun, the giver of all life and highest consciousness. Nowadays we often use fire in ceremonies by lighting a candle to bring light into the dark, or by making a fire in a fireplace. We light votive candles in churches as we pray for divine intervention for our loved ones. I find deep satisfaction in meditating while gazing into the flames of a fire. Communal gathering around a fire is an ancient social tradition.

You can bring the highest consciousness in the form of light into your cleansing and energizing ritual by lighting a candle.

Conducting Your Cleansing Ritual

After choosing representations of the four elements, you should create a personalized setting. I use a small table set with beautiful things that are meaningful for me. You might use a beautiful colored cloth, a bowl of water, a flower, some sand or soil, incense, a statue or picture representing the divine, a candle, a crystal, a feather, or whatever has power and meaning for you.

You can begin your ritual by blessing the water, lighting the incense, and invoking the help and guidance of a higher power that you relate to best. This might be a calling out for your own highest self, God, Jesus, Mother Mary, Buddha, personal guides, angels, your guru or teacher, or simply the divine intelligence. Then you can state your intention of cleaning the piece of jewelry of all negative energies and dip it into the bowl of water; wave it through the incense and the flame; and lay it down and sprinkle some sand or soil on it.

Next you should concentrate on your intentions and the healing and transforming energy that you would like to receive through your new piece of jewelry. Express those wishes out loud. Name the personal challenges in your life that you want to address with the help of this piece. Hold the piece in your left hand, hold your right hand over it, breathe deeply, and focus on the energy of the piece. Then release your breath rapidly.

Now your Soul Jewelry is charged and ready to serve your highest good and goals.

The Power of Intention

The above ritual may remind you of Neurolinguistic Programming, discussed in Chapter 5. Through the ritual you are programming your highest wishes and values into your own unconscious mind with the jewelry piece as the anchor. For example, you might express your intention to always act from your heart, to be grateful for the riches you have, or to be more compassionate toward yourself and others. By programming these intentions into a gemstone or jewelry item, you invite grace and the divine to participate in your efforts and endow the object with manifold power.

You can use this technique to imbue a piece of jewelry that you give as a gift with specific wishes from your heart and soul. In this way your feelings of love, appreciation, and commitment and your best wishes for the person's well-being will be held in an almost eternal vessel.

And now simply enjoy!

A Farewell As You Set Off

If you picked up this book, it was because you feel some stirring inside yourself to have a deeper understanding of some of the mysteries of your life: Why do things happen as they do in your life? How did you come to this place where you are at present? What is the path unfolding before you, and how can you get where you want to go? How can you move around some of the obstacles that have slowed you down in the past?

This inner voice that you are hearing is your longing to connect with spiritual wisdom, with your greater purpose and place in the universe, with the divine. You are not alone in your quest. There are many sources of wisdom that can guide you. Gemstones and crystals can offer you both physical support through their healing energies, and emotional and spiritual support by reminding you of the life themes that you want to attend to at this stage of your journey. And, of course, their immense beauty is a source of pleasure throughout your day.

I hope that this book has inspired you to look more deeply into your relationship to the cosmos, the course of your life, and your personality. It is possible for you to take charge of your life by harnessing the ancient wisdom of astrology and the healing energy of beautiful gemstones and crystals.

If I have piqued your interest about astrology with this brief intro-
duction, you might wish to learn more about it through reading or
seminars. Whenever I hit an obstacle on my path, I use astrology to
help me find deeper insight into the principles underlying the obstacle.
Astrology helps me to stay calm but also empowers me to action during transitions from an outdated self that no longer serves me to a new
self. Astrology is simply a means of achieving consciousness and sensing the divine presence in your life.

Now that you are armed with this wisdom, I would like to invite
you to accept the challenge of taking the next steps on your spiritual
journey. Though your exact path cannot be known at this time, be
secure in the knowledge that you are never alone and that the cosmos
wishes your well being. I wish you Godspeed on your journey into
your own inner sanctuary and a multitude of joyous experiences and
many blessings with your new friends, the precious gems in your life.

Free Catalog

Get the latest information on our body, mind, and spirit products! To receive a **free** copy of Llewellyn's consumer catalog, *New Worlds of Mind & Spirit,* simply call 1-877-NEW-WRLD or visit our website at www.llewellyn.com and click on *New Worlds.*

LLEWELLYN ORDERING INFORMATION

Order Online:
Visit our website at www.llewellyn.com, select your books, and order them on our secure server.

Order by Phone:
- Call toll-free within the U.S. at 1-877-NEW-WRLD (1-877-639-9753). Call toll-free within Canada at 1-866-NEW-WRLD (1-866-639-9753)
- We accept VISA, MasterCard, and American Express

Order by Mail:
Send the full price of your order (MN residents add 6.5% sales tax) in U.S. funds, plus postage & handling to:

Llewellyn Worldwide
2143 Wooddale Drive, Dept. 978-0-7387-1443-1
Woodbury, MN 55125-2989

Postage & Handling:
Standard (U.S., Mexico, & Canada). If your order is:
$24.99 and under, add $3.00
$25.00 and over, FREE STANDARD SHIPPING

AK, HI, PR: $15.00 for one book plus $1.00 for each additional book.

International Orders (airmail only):
$16.00 for one book plus $3.00 for each additional book

Orders are processed within 2 business days.
Please allow for normal shipping time. Postage and handling rates subject to change.

Astrology for Beginners

A Simple Way to Read Your Chart

JOANN HAMPAR

Getting a glimpse of your own astrological chart isn't a challenge these days. The tough part is finding meaning in this complex diagram of symbols.

In *Astrology for Beginners*, Joann Hampar shows that interpreting your birth chart is actually easy. Emphasizing a practical approach, this step-by-step guide takes you effortlessly through the language of astrological symbols. As each chapter unfolds, a new realm of your horoscope will be revealed, including chart patterns, zodiac signs, houses, planets, and aspects. By the last lesson, you'll be able to read and interpret your chart—what originally looked like a jumble of symbols—and gain valuable insight into yourself and others.

978-0-7387-1106-5
216 pp., 6 x 9   **$14.95**

To order, call 1-877-NEW-WRLD
Prices subject to change without notice

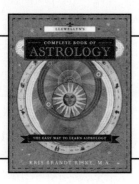

Llewellyn's Complete Book of Astrology

The Easy Way to Learn Astrology

KRIS BRANDT RISKE, M.A.

The horoscope is filled with insights into personal traits, talents, and life possibilities. With *Llewellyn's Complete Book of Astrology*, you can learn to read and understand this amazing cosmic road map for yourself and others.

Professional astrologer Kris Brandt Riske introduces the many mysterious parts that make up the horoscope, devoting special attention to three popular areas of interest: relationships, career, and money. Friendly and easy to follow, this comprehensive book guides you to explore the zodiac signs, planets, houses, and aspects, and teaches how to synthesize this valuable information. Riske also explores the history of astrology going back to the ancient Babylonians, in addition to the different branches of contemporary astrology.

Once you learn the language of astrology, you'll be able to read birth charts of yourself and others, determine compatibility between two people, track your earning potential, uncover areas of opportunity or challenge, and analyze your career path.

978-0-7387-1071-6
360 pp., 8 x 10 $18.95

To order, call 1-877-NEW-WRLD
Prices subject to change without notice

The Complete Book of
Spiritual Astrology
PER HENRIK GULLFOSS

There is an excellent tool to map the spirit's voyage toward enlightenment—astrology. Bestselling Norwegian author Per Henrik Gullfoss introduces this fascinating dimension of astrology—charting the evolution of the soul according to the planets.

Both beginners and professional astrologers can use this easy-to-understand guide to spiritual astrology. Gullfoss introduces the signs, planets, elements, modalities, houses, aspects, and other components of the birth chart, and then explores each from an evolutionary perspective. See how each facet of the horoscope offers clues for transitioning from ego consciousness to soul consciousness. Understand the role of love, wisdom, beauty, and joy in your life. Discover what your soul seeks to experience and express on its earthly journey, the gifts and challenges for this lifetime, as well as what must be mastered to achieve enlightenment.

978-0-7387-1258-1
264 pp., 6 x 9   **$24.95**

To order, call 1-877-NEW-WRLD
Prices subject to change without notice

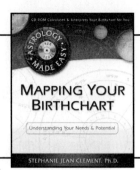

Mapping Your Birthchart

Understanding Your Needs and Potential

STEPHANIE JEAN CLEMENT, PH.D.

You know your "sign," but that's just the tip of the astrological iceberg. You've got a moon sign, a rising sign, and loads of other factors in your astrological makeup. Together they form the complete picture of you as an individual: your desires, talents, emotions . . . and your public persona and your private needs.

Mapping Your Birthchart removes the mystery from astrology so you can look at any chart and get a basic understanding of the person behind it. Learn the importance of the planets, the different signs of the zodiac, and how they relate to your everyday life. Stephanie Jean Clement introduces the basics of the astrology chart, devotes a chapter to each planet—with information about signs, houses, and aspects— provides simple explanations of astrological and psychological factors, and includes examples from the charts of well-known people including Tiger Woods, Celine Dion, and George W. Bush.

The free CD-ROM included with this book allows you to calculate and interpret your birthchart, and print out astrological reports and charts for yourself, your family, and friends.

978-0-7387-0202-5
240 pp., 7½ x 9⅛, includes CD-ROM $21.95

To order, call 1-877-NEW-WRLD
Prices subject to change without notice

Crystals for Beginners

A Guide to Collecting &
Using Stones & Crystals

CORRINE KENNER

Revered for their beauty, unique electrical qualities, and metaphysical attributes, crystals have been precious to mankind for centuries. *Crystals for Beginners* explores the universal allure of crystals and demonstrates how to channel their dynamic energies.

Beginning with how crystals were formed in the Earth billions of years ago, this practical guide introduces the history and myth surrounding these powerful minerals. From agates to zoisite, the characteristics of specific crystals are presented, along with advice for collecting, cleansing, and charging them. Readers also learn how to apply crystal energy to meditation, healing, psychic development, magic, divination, astral projection, dream work, and much more.

978–0–7387–0755–6
264 pp., 5³⁄₁₆ x 8   **$12.95**

To order, call 1-877-NEW-WRLD
Prices subject to change without notice